Journey to
Gold Mountain

The Asian American Experience

Spacious Dreams
   The First Wave of Asian Immigration

Journey to Gold Mountain
   The Chinese in Nineteenth Century America

Raising Cane
   The World of Plantation Hawaii

Issei and Nisei
   The Settling of Japanese America

From the Land of Morning Calm
   The Koreans in America

Ethnic Islands
   The Emergence of Urban Chinese America

In the Heart of Filipino America
   Immigrants from the Pacific Isles

India in the West
   South Asians in America

Democracy and Race
   Asian Americans and World War II

Strangers at the Gates Again
   Asian American Immigration After 1965

From Exiles to Immigrants
   The Refugees from Southeast Asia

Breaking Silences
   Asian Americans Today

Lives of Famous Asian Americans
   Arts/Entertainment/Sports

Lives of Famous Asian Americans
   Business/Science/Politics

Lives of Famous Asian Americans
   Literature and Education

Journey to Gold Mountain

THE CHINESE IN 19TH-CENTURY AMERICA

Ronald Takaki

PROFESSOR OF ETHNIC STUDIES
THE UNIVERSITY OF CALIFORNIA AT BERKELEY

Adapted by Rebecca Stefoff

Chelsea House Publishers

New York Philadelphia

On the cover A Chinese gold miner in
California in the late 19th century.

Chelsea House Publishers

EDITORIAL DIRECTOR   Richard Rennert
EXECUTIVE MANAGING EDITOR   Karyn Gullen Browne
COPY CHIEF   Robin James
PICTURE EDITOR   Adrian G. Allen
ART DIRECTOR   Robert Mitchell
MANUFACTURING DIRECTOR   Gerald Levine
PRODUCTION COORDINATOR   Marie Claire Cebrián-Ume

The Asian American Experience

SENIOR EDITOR   Jake Goldberg
SERIES DESIGN   Marjorie Zaum

Staff for *Journey To Gold Mountain*

COPY EDITOR   Nicole Greenblatt
EDITORIAL ASSISTANT   Kelsey Goss
PICTURE RESEARCHER   Wendy P. Wills

Adapted and reprinted from *Strangers from a Different Shore,*
© 1989 by Ronald Takaki, by arrangement with the author and
Little Brown and Company, Inc.

Library of Congress Cataloging-in-Publication Data
Takaki, Ronald T., 1939–
   Journey to Gold Mountain: the Chinese in nineteenth-century
America / Ronald Takaki.
      p. cm.—(Asian American experience)
   Includes bibliographical references and index.
ISBN 0-7910-2177-7
      0-7910-2277-3 (pbk.)
   1. Chinese Americans—History—19th century—Juvenile litera-
ture. I. Title. II. Series: Asian American experience (New York, N.Y.)
E184.C5T35 1994   93-4649
973'.04951—dc20   CIP
                                                  AC

Contents

Introduction by Ronald Takaki   7

Map of Asia   15

1 Searching for Gold Mountain   17

2 Building the Mighty Transcontinental Railroad   29

3 The Garden of California   41

4 The "Chinese Laundryman"   49

5 Mississippi Fields and Massachusetts Factories   55

6 "The Heathen Chinee"   65

7 The Chinese Struggle for Civil Rights   81

8 Putting Down Roots   91

9 Chinese Women in America   101

10 A World of Bachelors   111

Chronology   120

Further Reading   122

Index   124

The Fish Dealer's Daughter *by Arnold Genthe, who took many haunting photographs of California's early Chinese communities. The girl wears gloves to protect her hands as she carries the family's wicker shrimp baskets. Chinese fishing villages along the California coast provided seafood for restaurants and stores in San Francisco's Chinatown.*

From a Different Shore

AS A CHILD IN HAWAII, I GREW UP IN A MULTICULTURAL corner of America. My own family had roots in Japan and China.

Grandfather Kasuke Okawa arrived in Hawaii in 1866, and my father, Toshio Takaki, came as a 13-year-old boy in 1918. My stepfather, Koon Keu Young, sailed from China to the islands when he was a teenager.

My neighbors were Japanese, Chinese, Hawaiian, Filipino, Portuguese, and Korean. Behind my house, Alice Liu and her friends played the traditional Chinese game of mahjongg late into the night, the clicking of the tiles lulling me to sleep.

Next to us the Miuras flew billowing and colorful carp kites on Japanese boy's day. I heard voices with different accents, different languages, and saw children of different colors.

Together we went barefoot to school and played games like baseball and *jan ken po*. We spoke "pidgin English," a melodious language of the streets and community. "Hey, da kind tako ono, you know," we would say, combining English, Japanese, and Hawaiian. "This octopus is delicious." Racially and culturally diverse, we all thought of ourselves as Americans.

But we did not know why families representing such an array of nationalities from different shores were living together and sharing their cultures and a common language. Our teachers and textbooks did not explain the diversity of our community or the sources of our unity.

7

After graduation from high school, I attended a college in a midwestern town where I found myself invited to "dinners for foreign students" sponsored by local churches and clubs like the Rotary. I politely tried to explain to my kind hosts that I was not a "foreign student." My fellow students and even my professors would ask me how long I had been in America and where I had learned to speak English. "In this country," I would reply. And sometimes I would add: "I was born in America, and my family has been here for three generations."

Asian Americans have been here for over 150 years. They are diverse, coming originally from countries such as China, Japan, Korea, the Philippines, India, Vietnam, Laos, and Cambodia. Many of them live in Chinatowns, the colorful streets filled with sidewalk vegetable stands and crowds of people carrying shopping bags; their communities are also called Little Tokyo, Koreatown, and Little Saigon. Asian Americans work in hot kitchens and bus tables in restaurants with elegant names like Jade Pagoda and Bombay Spice. In garment factories, Chinese and Korean women hunch over whirling sewing machines, their babies sleeping nearby on blankets. In the Silicon Valley of California, rows and rows of Vietnamese and Laotian women serve as the eyes and hands of production assembly lines for computer chip industries. Tough Chinese gang members strut on Grant Avenue in San Francisco and Canal Street in New York's Chinatown. In La Crosse, Wisconsin, Hmong refugees from Laos, now dependent on welfare, sit and stare at the snowdrifts outside their windows. Asian American engineers do complex research in the laboratories of the high-technology industries along

Route 128 in Massachusetts. Asian Americans seem to be everywhere on university campuses.

Today, Asian Americans belong to the fastest growing ethnic group in the United States. Kept out of the United States by immigration restriction laws in the 19th and early 20th centuries, Asians have recently been coming again to America. The 1965 immigration act reopened the gates to immigrants from Asia, allowing 20,000 immigrants from each country to enter every year. In the early 1990s, half of all immigrants entering annually are Asian.

The growth of the Asian-American population has been dramatic: In 1960, there were only 877,934 Asians in the United States, representing a mere one half of 1% of the American people. Thirty years later, they numbered about seven million or 3% of the population. They included 1,645,000 Chinese, 1,400,000 Filipinos, 845,000 Japanese, 815,000 Asian Indians, 800,000 Koreans, 614,000 Vietnamese, 150,000 Laotians, 147,000 Cambodians, and 90,000 Hmong. By the year 2000, Asian Americans will probably represent 4% of the total United States population. In California, Asian Americans already make up 10% of the state's inhabitants, compared with 7.5% for African Americans.

Yet very little is known about Asian Americans and their history. Many existing history books give Asian Americans only passing notice—or overlook them entirely. "When one hears Americans tell of the immigrants who built this nation," Congressman Norman Mineta of California observed, "one is often led to believe that all our forebearers came from Europe. When one hears stories about the pioneers going West to shape the land, the Asian immigrant is rarely mentioned."

Indeed, many history books have equated "American" with "white" or "European" in origin. In his prize-winning study, *The Uprooted*, Harvard historian Oscar Handlin presented—to use the book's subtitle—"the Epic Story of the Great Migrations that Made the American People." But Handlin's "epic story" completely left out the "uprooted" from lands across the Pacific Ocean and the "great migrations" from Asia that also helped to make "the American people." As Americans, we have origins in Europe, the Americas, Africa, and also Asia.

We need to include Asians in the history of America. How and why, we ask in this series, were the experiences of these various groups—Chinese, Japanese, Korean, Filipino, Asian Indian, and Southeast Asian—similar to and different from each other? Comparing the experiences of different nationalities can help us see what events were particular to a group and also highlight the experiences they all shared.

Why did Asian immigrants leave everything they knew and loved to come to a strange world so far away? They were "pushed" by hardships in the homelands and "pulled" by demands for their labor in Canada, Brazil, and especially the United States. But what were their own fierce dreams—from the first enterprising Chinese miners of the 1850s in search of "Gold Mountain" to the recent refugees fleeing frantically on helicopters and leaking boats from the ravages of war in Vietnam?

Besides their points of origin, we need to examine the experiences of Asian Americans in different geographical regions, especially Hawaii compared with the mainland. The time of arrival also shaped their lives and communities. About one million people entered the United States between the California gold rush of 1849 and the 1924 immigration act that cut off the flow of peoples from Asian countries. After a break of some 40 years, a second group numbering about four million came between 1965 and 1990. How do we compare the two waves of Asian immigration?

To answer our questions in these volumes, we must study Asian Americans as men and women with minds, wills, and voices. By "voices" we mean their own words and stories as told in their oral histories, conversations, speeches, and songs as well as their own writings—diaries, letters, newspapers, novels, and poems. We need to know the ordinary people.

So much of history has been the story of kings and elites, as if the "little people" were invisible and voiceless. An Asian American told an interviewer: "I am a second generation Korean American without any achievements in life and I have no education. What is it you want to hear from me? My life is not worth telling to anyone." Similarly, a Chinese immigrant said: "You know, it seems to me there's no use in me telling you all this! I was just a simple worker, a farm worker around here. My story is not going to interest anybody." But others realize they are worthy of attention. "What is it you want to know?" an old Filipino immigrant asked a researcher. "Talk about history. What's that . . . ah, the story of my life . . . and how people lived with each other in my time."

Their stories can enable us to understand Asians as actors in the making of history and as people entitled to dignity. "I hope this survey do a lot of good for Chinese people," a Chinese man told an interviewer from Stanford

University in the 1920s. "Make American people realize that Chinese people are humans. I think very few American people really know anything about Chinese." Elderly Asians want the younger generations to know about their experiences. "Our stories should be listened to by many young people," said a 91-year-old retired Japanese plantation laborer. "It's for their sake. We really had a hard time, you know."

The stories of Asian immigrations belong to our country's history. They need to be recorded in our history books, for they reflect the making of America as a nation of immigrants, as a place where men and women came to find a new beginning. At first, many Asian immigrants—probably most of them—saw themselves as sojourners, or temporary migrants. Like many European immigrants such as the Italians and Greeks, they came to America thinking they would be here only a short time. They had left their wives and children behind in their homelands. Their plan was to work here for a few years and then return home with money. But, after their arrival, many found themselves staying. They became settlers instead of remaining sojourners. Bringing their families to their adopted country, they began putting down new roots in America.

But, coming here from Asia, many of America's immigrants found they were not allowed to feel at home in the United States. Even their grandchildren and great-grandchildren still find they are not viewed and accepted as Americans. "We feel that we're a guest in someone else's house," said third generation Ron Wakabayashi, National Director of the Japanese American Citizens League, "that we can never really relax and put our feet on the table."

Behind Wakabayashi's complaint is the question: Why have Asian Americans been considered outsiders? America's immigrants from Pacific shores found they were forced to remain strangers in the new land. Their experiences here were profoundly different from the experiences of European immigrants. Asian immigrants had qualities they could not change or hide—the shape of their eyes, the color of their hair, the complexion of their skins. They were subjected not only to cultural and ethnic prejudice but also to racism. Unlike the Irish and other groups from Europe, Asian immigrants were not treated as individuals but as members of a group with distinctive physical characteristics. Regardless of their personal merits, they sadly discovered, they could not gain acceptance in the larger society.

Unlike European immigrants, Asians were victimized by laws and policies that discriminated on the basis of race. The Chinese Exclusion Act of 1882 barred the Chinese from coming to America because they were Chinese. The National Origins Act of 1924 totally prohibited Japanese immigration.

The laws determined not only who could come to America but also who could become citizens. Decades before Asian immigration began, the United States had already defined the complexion of its citizens: the Naturalization Law of 1790 had specified that naturalized citizenship was to be reserved for "whites." This law remained in effect until 1952. Unlike white ethnic immigrants from countries like Ireland, Asian immigrants were denied citizenship and also the right to vote.

But America also had an opposing tradition and vision, springing from the reality of racial and cultural "diversity." Ours has been, as Walt Whitman celebrated so lyrically, "a teeming Nation of nations" composed of a "vast, surging, hopeful army of workers," a new society where all should be welcomed, "Chinese, Irish, German,—all, all, without exceptions." In the early 20th century, a Japanese immigrant described in poetry a lesson that had been learned by farm laborers of different nationalities—Japanese, Filipino, Mexican, and Asian Indian:

> *People harvesting*
> *Work together unaware*
> *Of racial problems.*

A Filipino immigrant laborer in California expressed a similar hope and understanding. America was, Macario Bulosan told his brother Carlos, "not a land of one race or one class of men" but "a new world" of respect and unconditional opportunities for all who toiled and suffered from oppression, from "the first Indian that offered peace in Manhattan to the last Filipino pea pickers." Asian immigrants came here, as one of them expressed it, searching for "a door into America" and seeking "to build a new life with untried materials." He asked: "Would it be possible for an immigrant like me to become a part of the American dream?"

This series invites students to learn how Asian Americans belong to the larger story of the rich multicultural mosaic called the United States of America.

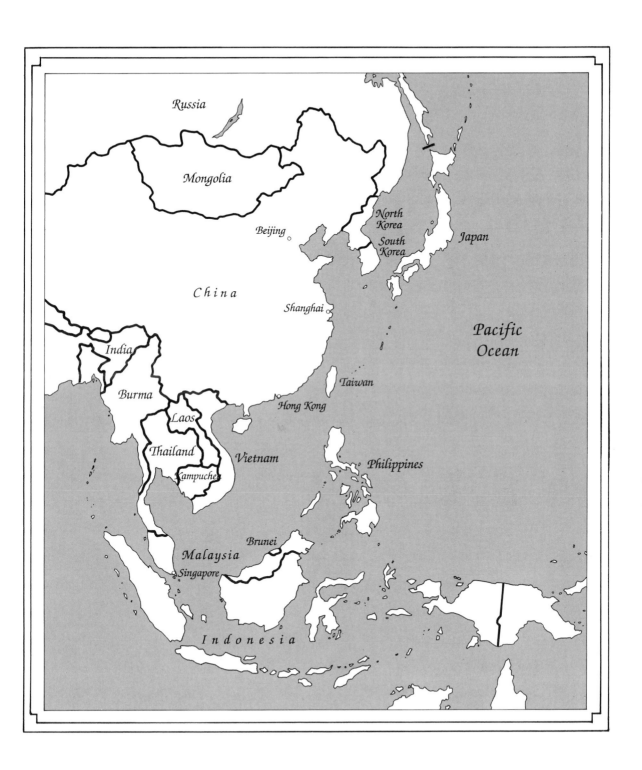

A butcher and grocery store in San Francisco's old Chinatown. Such stores not only provided immigrants with the foods they were accustomed to, but served as centers of social life within the Chinese American community.

Chapter One

Searching for Gold Mountain

ONE SUMMER DAY IN THE 1850s, A TRAVELER IN THE Sierra Nevada mountains of California came upon an interesting sight. In the harsh landscape of tumbled brown rocks he saw "long files of Chinamen working alone." The traveler enjoyed seeing the Chinese men; they broke up "the monotony of the landscape." They wore blue cotton shirts, wide-legged trousers, wooden shoes, and broad-brimmed straw hats. In the Chinese fashion of the time, their jet-black hair was cut short, except in back, where each man wore a long braid called a queue.

The men were busy sifting sand from the beds of mountain streams, rocking it back and forth in shallow pans as the water ran out. Like many other people in California in those years, the Chinese miners were panning for gold.

Gold had been discovered in 1848 along the American River in California, on the property of a man named John Sutter. Although Sutter tried to keep the discovery a secret, word of the fabulous find soon reached San Francisco, and hundreds of people deserted the city to set off for the American River. The news spread to the rest of the United States, and to other parts of the world as well. By January of 1849, 60 ships and thousands of overland travelers were headed for California. The California gold rush had begun.

More than 70,000 hopeful adventurers embarked for California in 1849 alone. Among these "Forty-Niners" were 325 men from China. More Chinese came the next year, and the next. Like the prospectors who came from the eastern United States and elsewhere, the Chinese hoped to find a fortune waiting for them in the California hills. A few of them *did* find gold—but all of them found a new world and a new way of life, with challenges, fears, and opportunities that they had not expected.

The Chinese were the first Asian group to enter America. What happened to them set a pattern for the way other Asians would be treated in America. They came to be seen as outsiders, as "strangers" who would not be allowed to become true Americans. Other Asian migrants would later be viewed this way, too. Japanese, Koreans, Filipinos, and East Indians would later meet the same barriers that the Chinese encountered. Today, Vietnamese, Cambodian, and Hmong refugees from war-torn Southeast Asia are still struggling to overcome these barriers. The history of all Asian immigrants echoes the story of the Chinese who came to America in the 19th century.

Most of the first wave of Chinese migrants came from Guangdong, a province on China's south coast. They were fleeing from turmoil and poverty. In the mid-19th century, Guangdong was torn by two wars between China and Britain, as well as by widespread rebellions, ethnic strife, and endless village and family feuds. The Chinese imperial government had raised taxes, and farmers who were unable to pay their taxes had to sell their land.

At the same time, Guangdong's population was rapidly growing. The province could not produce enough rice to feed its people, especially when frequent floods destroyed the crops. A visitor to China in 1852 reported that "the least failure of the rice crop produces wretchedness."

Living in these hopeless conditions, people listened eagerly to tales of gold beyond the Pacific Ocean. They called

Emigrants in a Chinese port prepare to board a ship bound for Gam Saan, *or "Gold Mountain." Thousands fled poverty in China to seek their fortunes in the gold fields of California.*

California *Gam Saan,* or "Gold Mountain." To them it seemed a land of unbelievable richness. They longed to go there, make their fortunes, and return triumphantly to China. In 1848, shortly after the discovery of gold at John Sutter's mill in California, a young man in Guangdong wrote to his brother, who was living in Boston. He said, "Good many Americans speak of California. Oh! Very rich country! I hear good many Americans and Europeans go there. Oh! They find gold very quickly, so I hear." He added, "I shall go there soon, I think."

The exciting news about Gold Mountain spread throughout China, filling people with the desire to join the gold rush. One traveler in China said that if everyone who wanted to go to California had been able to afford it, whole Chinese towns would have been emptied. A popular Chinese saying of the time promised that if a man could not get a thousand dollars in California, he would surely get at least eight hundred. But even with only three hundred dollars he could return to China and become "a big, very big gentleman."

19

A folk song told of the restless optimism that inspired these adventurers:

> *In the second reign year of Haamfung [1852], a trip*
> *to Gold Mountain was made.*
> *With a pillow on my shoulder, I began my perilous*
> *journey:*
> *Sailing a boat with bamboo poles across the sea,*
> *Leaving behind wife and sisters in search of money,*
> *No longer lingering with the woman in the bedroom,*
> *No longer paying respect to parents at home.*

The Chinese who went to California were called *gam saan haak*, "travelers to Gold Mountain." Americans often called them "Celestials," from an old name for China: the Celestial Empire. Although this term was not an insult, it sometimes had a rather mocking, belittling tone.

Americans also called the Chinese "coolies." Coolies were unfree laborers who were kidnapped, forced, or tricked into leaving their homes and made to work in a foreign country against their wills. Thousands of Chinese *were* forced into coolie labor in places such as Cuba and Peru, but few, if any, of the Chinese in California were coolies. William Speer, a missionary in San Francisco's Chinatown for decades beginning in the 1850s, never found evidence that any Chinese laborers had been brought to America and used as slaves against their will. Instead, most of the Chinese migrants came to America on the credit-ticket system. Under this system, a broker would loan money to a migrant to buy his ticket, and the migrant would in turn repay the loan, plus interest, out of his earnings in the new country.

The 325 Chinese who joined the gold rush in 1849 were just the beginning. The next year, 450 more Chinese arrived in California. Then suddenly they came in greater numbers: 2,716 in 1851, and 20,026 in 1852. By 1870, there were 63,000 Chinese in the United States. Although they could be found throughout the country, most of them—77%—were in California.

The "Old West" has become an American folk legend. The phrase calls up images of cowboys and Indians, sheriffs and outlaws. But there were also many Chinese faces in the Old West, and their presence has often been overlooked. In some western states, Chinese people made up a significant share of the population: 29% in Idaho, 10% in Montana, and 9% in California. Nearly all of the Chinese were adult men, and their contribution to the economy was important. In California, a quarter of the total work force in the late 19th century was Chinese.

Chinese communities in America during the 19th century were diverse and changing. At first, the Chinese lived mostly in the countryside. Then, between 1870 and 1900, they became more urban. They lived in San Francisco, which they called *Dai Fou* ("Big City") and in Sacramento (*Yee Fou*, or "Second City"), Stockton (*Sam Fou*, or "Third City"), Marysville, and Los Angeles. During these years, the Chinese also spread out across America. In 1870, more than three-quarters of all the Chinese in the United States lived in California. By 1900, only half of them lived in California. Thousands of Chinese had settled in New England and the Mid-Atlantic states. They formed the beginnings of Chinatowns in Boston and New York City.

Chinese laborers in a Colorado mine. Mining that involved tunneling and blasting was hard and dangerous work.

The first Chinese who came to America worked as miners. Later, the Chinese practiced a wide range of occupations. In the cities, there were Chinese merchants, shopkeepers, professionals, craftspeople, and laborers. In the countryside, most Chinese were farm laborers or service workers such as cooks and house servants, although there were also Chinese merchants and independent farmers.

The people of California welcomed the Chinese at first. "Quite a large number of the Celestials have arrived among us of late, enticed thither by the golden romance that has filled the world," a California newspaper reported in 1852. The paper predicted that the Chinese would someday become U.S. citizens, saying "the China boys will yet vote at the same polls, study at the same schools and bow at the same altar as our own countrymen."

Three years later, San Francisco merchant Lai Chun-Chuen observed that the Chinese "were received like guests" and "greeted with favor" in America. He said that the Chinese and Americans treated each other politely: "From far and near we came and were pleased."

Lai and his fellow travelers to Gold Mountain had reason to be pleased. For a while, it seemed that the Chinese newcomers were going to be accepted as part of American society. When California became a state in 1850, the Chinese shared in the celebration ceremonies, along with American citizens. Happily acknowledging the presence of the Chinese and other foreigners in California, a state judge declared, "Born and reared under different Governments and speaking different tongues, we nevertheless meet here to-day as brothers. . . . You stand among us in all respects as equals. . . . Henceforth we have one country, one hope, one destiny."

In August of that same year, the mayor of San Francisco invited the Chinese to join the citizens of the city in a memorial for the late President Zachary Taylor. Two members of the Chinese community wrote to the mayor, "The China Boys feel proud of the distinction you have shown them, and will always endeavor to merit your good opinion and the good opinion of the citizens of their adopted country."

Two years later, the Chinese helped celebrate George Washington's birthday in San Francisco. At the parade, one onlooker noticed "some two hundred Celestials, or, as their banner termed them 'China boys of San Francisco.'" The same observer called the Chinese "our most orderly and industrious citizens." The Chinese future in America looked bright. In January 1852, Governor John McDougal of California declared that more Chinese migrants would be needed to help drain the state's swamplands. He praised the Chinese as "one of the most worthy classes of our newly adopted citizens—to whom the climate and the character of these lands are peculiarly suited."

But Governor McDougal failed to see that public opinion was fast turning against the Chinese. "California for Americans" was a rallying cry of the nativist movement, an antiforeigner backlash that gained strength in the United States in the second half of the 19th century. Nativists believed that there were too many foreigners in the country, and that the Chinese immigrants were a threat to "real Americans." According to the nativists, the Chinese took jobs that should have been held by Americans, and they brought customs and values that were alien to "the American way."

Many white miners in California shared this hostility toward foreigners. They wanted to drive the French, Mexicans, Hawaiians, Chileans, and especially the Chinese out of the gold fields. These miners demanded that the state eliminate competition from foreign miners.

The state government, now headed by a new governor named John Bigler, listened to the white miners' demands. A committee of the state legislature claimed that the well-being of the mining districts was threatened by "vast numbers of the Asiatic races, and of the inhabitants of the Pacific Islands, and of many others dissimilar from ourselves in customs, language and education." The committee said that most Asian laborers were "servile contract laborers" who did not intend to become American citizens. The presence of Chinese workers, claimed the committee, lowered the wages and living standards of the white American workers in California and discouraged other white Americans from coming to the state. To halt this threat, the committee recommended a tax on foreign miners. The governor agreed that the state should do what it could to keep the Chinese out. To halt the "tide of Asiatic immigration," he called for a ban on contract labor and for heavy taxes on the Chinese in California.

The California legislature responded in May of 1852 by passing the foreign miners' license tax. This tax was aimed mainly at the Chinese miners. It required every foreign miner who did not choose to become a U.S. citizen to pay $3 a month to the state. The tax discriminated against the Chinese in particular, for even if they had wanted to become citizens, they could not do so. A federal law from 1790 declared that only "white" persons could become naturalized citizens.

The foreign miners' tax remained in force until it was canceled by the federal Civil Rights Act of 1870. By then California had collected $5 million from the Chinese—about a third of the state's total income. But the purpose of the foreign miners' tax was not to raise money; it was to discourage the Chinese from coming to California. Other laws were passed for the same purpose. In 1855, California passed a law that required the master or owner of a ship to pay a landing tax of $50 for each passenger who was not eligible to become a citizen—in other words, for each nonwhite passenger. This law was intended to discourage ship masters from accepting Chinese passengers.

Most Chinese miners worked placer claims. As independent prospectors or in small partnerships, they panned for gold dust and nuggets in the streams of the Sierra Nevada foothills.

Despite the obstacle of the license tax, most of the Chinese in California during the 1850s and 1860s were miners. Generally, they were independent prospectors. Sometimes as many as 40 partners banded together to form small companies. They staked claims to parcels of land where they hoped to find gold, usually along rivers. Thus in 1856 Ah Louie and Company claimed 240 feet at Buckeye Bar along the Yuba River, and Sham Kee claimed 4,200 feet along the same river eight miles outside of Marysville. Many of these companies did well, renewing their claims annually and often even purchasing them. Ah Chung and Company, for example, purchased two claims of 60 feet each, paying $620 for the claims, two wheelbarrows, and some lumber.

Chinese miners mostly worked placer claims. Placer mining means looking for gold nuggets or dust in rivers or on the surface of the ground, rather than tunneling or blasting for it. Placer miners would shovel sand from a stream into a pan or rocker, then carefully wash away the sand and dirt. The particles of gold, being heavy, would sink to the bottom of the pan. In this way, over time, immense quantities of sand were sifted—the equivalent of whole mountains. Most Chinese miners found only about $2 to $3 worth of gold dust a day. But some of them found richer claims.

Chinese miners became a common sight in the California foothills, especially along the Yuba River and its tributaries. A newspaper writer told of companies of 20 or 30 Chinese "inhabiting close cabins, so small that one . . . would not be of sufficient size to allow a couple of Americans to breathe in it. Chinamen, stools, tables, cooking utensils, bunks etc., all huddled up together in indiscriminate confusion, and enwreathed with dense smoke, presented a spectacle."

Day-to-day life for the Chinese miners was competitive and anxious. They had to protect themselves from "claim jumpers," people who challenged their right to their claims or simply stole their gold. Some of the telegrams that the Chinese miners sent from the mining community of Downieville captured their tension and worry. On March 2, 1874, a miner named Fong Sing sent this telegram to a Chinese company in San Francisco:

> Git Wo. I want you pay your cousin Ah Hoey
> expenses to come Downieville quick attend to claim.
> Am afraid there will be big fight. Answer.

Two days later Fong Sing sent another telegram:

> Trouble about mining claims. I owe a share and
> all the company want you come. I want you come.
> Ans yes or no.

That same month, Fong Wo and Company sent to San Francisco a terse telegram that hints at the pressures the miners felt:

> What the price of opium. Answer.

These Chinese men were lonely, far from their families. Their work was exhausting. The drug offered them an escape from the dreary realities of their lives. The sad truth was that most of those who came searching for Gold Mountain found only hard work and little reward.

Starting in 1852, foreign miners in California had to pay a tax every month. Meant to discourage Chinese immigrants from coming to the state, the foreign miners' tax was part of a growing anti-Chinese movement.

27

In 1869, the railway across the United States was completed when tracks from the East and West coasts met in Utah. Much of the historic triumph goes to the Chinese laborers who laid the western track through some of the most rugged terrain in the world.

Chapter Two

Building the Mighty Transcontinental Railroad

TO THE CHINESE, GOLD MOUNTAIN PROMISED NOT ONLY gold to be mined but also other job opportunities. In the port cities of China, leaflets distributed by labor brokers said, "Americans are very rich people. They want the Chinaman to come and make him very welcome. There you will have great pay, large houses, and food and clothing of the finest description. . . . Money is in great plenty and to spare in America."

In the mid-1860s, the profits from gold mining decreased because most of the easily obtainable gold had been found. The Chinese miners were leaving the gold fields, and they needed jobs. From independent miners who had worked for themselves, many Chinese immigrants now became wage earners who worked for bosses. By 1880, more than two-thirds of the Chinese in Sacramento City and Marysville were employed in white-owned businesses. This pattern continued as more Chinese moved out of mining and went to work in industry. But the shift from prospecting to earning wages did not discourage Chinese from coming to America. To the ordinary Chinese, America was still a land of opportunity—a Gold Mountain. In California during the 1860s, a Chinese laborer could work for the railroad and make $30 a month. This was 10 times as much as he would earn in China.

The railroad was a major source of jobs for Chinese workers. The United States was in the middle of a railroad boom, creating a national system of railways to carry freight and passengers. In the mid-19th century, one of the nation's most ambitious goals was to build a transcontinental line, a railroad that would connect the East and West coasts. The first rail lines from the East crossed the Mississippi River in 1852, opening the way for the railroads to enter the prairies. The next step was to lay track across the West.

Two railway companies competed in this venture. The Union Pacific company began laying track westward from Omaha, Nebraska. At the same time, the Central Pacific company laid track eastward from Sacramento, California. When the two lines met, the transcontinental railway would be complete. Each company wanted to cover more ground than the other—not just out of pride and competitiveness, but because they were being paid by the government for each mile of track they laid. The Central Pacific faced the biggest challenges. In the western part of the country, the railway had to cross a thousand miles or more of America's steepest mountains, deepest canyons, and most barren deserts. Laying this track was one of the great triumphs of 19th-century American industry. It was an achievement based on Chinese labor.

In February 1865, 50 Chinese workers were hired by the Central Pacific to work on the transcontinental line. Shortly afterward, 50 more Chinese were hired. Company president Leland Stanford praised the new laborers as "quiet, peaceable, industrious, economical—ready and apt to learn all the different kinds of work" involved in building a railroad. Company superintendent Charles Crocker said, "They prove nearly equal to white men in the amount of labor they perform, and are much more reliable."

Crocker was particularly happy that the Chinese did not seem inclined to go on strike—that is, to stop working as a way of getting higher wages or better working conditions. "No danger of strikes among them," he reported. "We are training them to all kinds of labor: blasting, driving horses, handling rock as well as pick and shovel."

When white workers demanded that the company stop hiring Chinese laborers, Crocker replied, "We can't get enough white labor to build this railroad, and build it we must, so we're forced to hire them. If you can't get along with them, we have only one alternative. We'll let you go and hire nobody but them." Within two years, the Central Pacific Railroad employed 12,000 Chinese laborers. Ninety percent of its entire work force was Chinese.

The company saved an enormous amount of money by using Chinese workers. The Chinese earned $31 a month and paid for their own food and lodging. White workers would have earned the same wages *plus* their food and lodging, which would have increased labor costs by one-third.

The Chinese workers who built the Central Pacific line performed heroic feats of labor. They cleared trees with saws and axes; they laid tracks with picks and shovels. They also did important technical jobs, such as operating power drills and handling explosives for blasting tunnels through the Donner Summit in the Sierra Nevada mountains. Sometimes the men had to work in baskets, hanging alongside sheer cliffs to lay explosive charges that blasted away whole mountainsides.

When they drilled through the Donner Summit, the Chinese workers were matched against some workers from Cornwall, a part of England that had produced generations of skilled tin and coal miners. Said superintendent Crocker, "We had a shaft down in the center. We were cutting both ways from the bottom of that shaft. . . . [We] got some Cornish miners and paid them extra wages. We put them into one side

Charles Crocker, superintendent of the Central Pacific company, hired the first Chinese railroad workers. Resentful white workers called them Crocker's Pets.

31

By 1867, 90% of the workers on the Central Pacific line were Chinese. Many of them performed important technical tasks. These men are drilling holes for explosive charges.

of the shaft . . . and we had Chinamen on the other side. We measured the work every Sunday morning; and the Chinamen without fail, always outmeasured the Cornish miners."

One observer described the Chinese workers as "a great army laying siege to Nature in her strongest citadel. The rugged mountains looked like stupendous ant-hills. They swarmed with Celestials, shoveling, wheeling, carting, drilling and blasting rocks and earth." The railway company wanted construction to move as fast as possible, since the company received a certain amount of land and money for every mile of track it built. While the Central Pacific was fighting its way eastward, the Union Pacific was hastening westward, and the competition grew keener.

To speed up construction, the Central Pacific managers forced the Chinese laborers to work through the winter of

1866. Snowdrifts more than 60 feet high covered the construction operations. The Chinese workers lived and worked in tunnels under the snow, with shafts to give them air and lanterns to light the way.

Snowslides occasionally buried camps and crews. In the spring, workers found the thawing corpses, still upright, their cold hands gripping shovels and picks and their mouths twisted in frozen terror. "The snow slides carried away our camps and we lost a good many men in those slides," a company official reported matter-of-factly. "Many of them we did not find until the next season when the snow melted."

The Chinese workers went on strike that spring. Demanding wages of $45 a month and an eight-hour day, 5,000 laborers walked out "as one man." The company offered to raise their wages from $31 to $35 a month, but the strikers turned down this offer and stood by their original demands. "Eight hours a day good for white men, all the same good for Chinamen," they declared. A San Francisco newspaper speculated that the strike had been drummed up by agents of the rival Union Pacific company. The newspaper writer could not believe that the Chinese strikers had minds and wills of their own, or that they were able to organize and take action to protect themselves without outside encouragement.

Meanwhile, the Central Pacific managers moved to break the strike. They sent telegrams to New York, asking if they could get 10,000 blacks to replace the striking Chinese. At the construction camps in the Sierra Nevada mountains, superintendent Crocker isolated the strikers and cut off their food supply. "I stopped the provisions on them," he stated, "stopped the butchers from butchering, and used such

33

With nothing more than picks, shovels, and wheelbarrows, Chinese laborers truly moved mountains, building trestle bridges and cutting and grading level pathways through the steep Sierra Nevada.

coercive measures." Coercion worked. Imprisoned in their camps in the Sierra Nevada and forced into starvation, the strikers surrendered within a week.

Beaten, the Chinese returned to work and completed the railroad. The importance of the Chinese contribution was widely admitted. One journalist, writing for the *Overland Monthly,* pointed out that the railroad fulfilled the hopes of many American leaders, including President Thomas Jefferson, who had sent Meriwether Lewis and William Clark to explore a westward route in 1804, and Thomas H. Benton, a senator who had wanted to see the United States stretch from ocean to ocean. Said the writer, "The dream of Thomas Jefferson and the desires of Thomas H. Benton's heart, have been wonderfully fulfilled. . . . But even they did not prophesy that Chinamen should build the Pacificward end of the road."

In 1869, the two railway lines met at Promontory Point, Utah. There Central Pacific president Leland Stanford hammered in a golden railroad spike. There were festive ceremonies in the Utah wilderness, with 1,500 people, including famous Americans from across the country, celebrating the historic moment. One witness captured the scene:

> One fact . . . forcibly impressed me at the laying of the last nail. Two lengths of rails, fifty-six feet, had been omitted. The Union Pacific people brought up their pair of rails, and the work of placing them was done by Europeans. The Central Pacific people then laid their pair of rails, the labor being performed by Mongolians [Chinese]. The foremen, in both cases, were Americans. Here, near the center of the American Continent, were the united efforts of repre-

sentatives of the continents of Europe, Asia, and America—America directing and controlling.

The immense job of building the transcontinental railroad was over. But with the task completed, thousands of Chinese laborers needed new jobs. Many of them went to San Francisco. In the years that followed, the Chinese community in San Francisco grew steadily, and so did the city's industries. Many factories and workshops employed Chinese workers. Like the transcontinental railroad, the industrial growth of San Francisco owed much to the Chinese.

In 1860, only 8% of the Chinese in California lived in San Francisco, compared with 70% in the mining districts. To new arrivals from China at this time, San Francisco was just a port of entry, a stop on their way to the gold fields. Ten years later, however, nearly one-fourth of California's Chinese people lived in San Francisco. Meanwhile, San Francisco had become a center of industry. In 1860, the city had about 200 manufacturing firms employing 1,500 workers. Ten years later, it had more than 12,000 industrial workers and was the country's ninth largest manufacturing city.

The Chinese who moved to San Francisco seeking jobs in the 1860s looked first to the Chinese community. An ethnic economy flourished, based on businesses run by the Chinese for the Chinese. Retail shops such as groceries, services such as hotels and laundries, vices such as gambling and prostitution, and entertainments such as theaters employed Chinese workers, but these businesses offered only a limited number of jobs. There was work elsewhere in the city, however, and Chinese laborers found jobs in San Francisco's key industries: boot and shoe manufacturing, wool production, tobacco processing and cigar making, and sewing. By 1872, nearly half the workingmen employed in the city's factories were Chinese.

The Chinese left the mining regions and entered San Francisco at a fortunate time. The Civil War (1861–65) had disrupted the flow of goods from factories in the East to markets in the West, opening up opportunities for San Fran-

The Central Pacific Railroad challenged the Union Pacific's record of 8 miles of track laid in a single day—Chinese workers from the Central Pacific set a new record, laying 10 miles of track in 12 hours.

Workers in a San Francisco cigar factory. The city's emergence as an industrial center was supported by Chinese labor.

ciscans to start their own factories. The local economy was growing, but Chinese workers found themselves concentrated in the low-wage industries. Cigar workers, for example, received only $287 in annual wages; 92% of them were Chinese. Tailors earned $588 a year, but only 9% were Chinese.

Chinese workers were also segregated within individual industries. In the garment industry, the Chinese worked mainly in factories that made women's clothing. They received an average yearly wage of $364. Workers who made men's clothing received $597 a year, but most of these workers were white. In factories where the labor force was racially mixed, whites occupied the skilled positions and Chinese the menial ones. White foremen directed Chinese crews. And even in cases where Chinese were assigned to the same tasks as whites, they were paid less than the whites. The work was equal, but the wages were not.

Although they discriminated against Chinese workers, employers knew how important the Chinese were to the industrial development of California. In an article called "How Our Chinamen Are Employed," a journalist named A. W. Loomis counted thousands of Chinese factory workers in woolen mills, knitting mills, paper mills, powder mills, tanneries, shoe factories, and garment industries. A San Francisco minister wrote an essay called *Chinaman or White Man, Which?* in which he said that California's industries could "not be maintained a single day" without low-paid Chinese labor.

California's prosperity depended on its Chinese workers. In 1876, the author of a book called *The Golden State* said, "In mining, farming, in factories and in the labor generally of California the employment of the Chinese has been found most desirable; and much of the labor done by these people if performed by white men at higher wages could not be continued nor made possible."

A vegetable seller in San Francisco. Agriculture was the livelihood of many Chinese—not just the farmers who grew the crops but also the vendors who distributed them.

Chapter Three

The Garden of California

NOT ALL OF THE CHINESE IN CALIFORNIA WORKED IN the mines, railroad crews, or factories. Many of them were found in the state's fields and orchards. They helped make California's Central Valley into one of the world's foremost garden spots.

California's agriculture was shifting from wheat farming to the cultivation of fruits and vegetables, and the Chinese played an important role in this change. The Chinese had a long history of agricultural knowledge. In their homeland, they had learned how to grow rice, fruit, and vegetables on every available bit of fertile land. In California, Chinese who had once farmed the Pearl River delta in Guangdong province shared their experience and knowledge with white farmers and growers. The Chinese, said one observer, "taught their over-lords how to plant, cultivate, and harvest orchard and garden crops."

The Chinese contribution to agriculture extended beyond California. In Oregon, a Chinese grower named Ah Bing bred the famous Bing cherry, and Lue Gim Gong in Florida developed the frost-resistant orange that gave the state its citrus industry.

But California was the heart of Chinese advances in agriculture. In the deltas of the San Joaquin and Sacramento rivers, the Chinese built irrigation systems similar to those that had been used along China's Yellow and Yangtze rivers for thousands of years. Wielding shovels, waist-deep in water, they drained swamps and marshes and transformed them into agricultural lands. Shovelful by shovelful, Chinese workers dug canals and built levees, the earthen dams that prevent fields from being flooded.

In 1869, a writer for the *Overland Monthly* magazine noted that the Chinese were changing California's landscape. He added that "the descendants of the people who drained those almost limitless marshes on either side of their own swiftly-flowing Yellow River, and turned them into luxuriant fields, are able to do the same thing on the banks of the Sacramento and the San Joaquin." In Salinas, Chinese laborers dug six miles of ditches to drain the land, cutting the peat soil "with huge knife-like spades and pitching it out with steel forks and hooks." Their work boosted the value of the land from $28 per acre in 1875 to $100 per acre two years later.

But the Chinese laborers wanted to be more than low-paid diggers. Many wanted to be farmers themselves, working the land for their own benefit. Some achieved this goal, especially in Sacramento, Yuba, and San Joaquin counties, the centers of agricultural development. The number of Chinese farmers and vegetable gardeners in these counties jumped from 119 in 1860 to 913 in 1880.

Most Chinese did not have the money to buy large tracts of land. However, they could enter the business of agriculture through tenant farming. Tenant farmers made agreements with white landowners. In exchange for the use of the land and equipment and the marketing of their crops, Chinese tenant farmers raised fruit and vegetables and then divided the profits with the landowners.

A deal made by Chou Ying and Wee Ying shows how tenant farming worked. In 1873, they signed a contract with landowner George D. Roberts, leasing 551 acres in three tracts. The lease stated that the Chinese tenant farmers would pay Roberts $8 per acre for one of the tracts. For the remaining two tracts, they would either give Roberts one-quarter of the crops or, if they chose to grow Chinese vegetables that would not sell well in white marketplaces, they would pay him $10 per acre.

Many of the Chinese tenant farming enterprises were partnerships, companies known as *yuen* (garden). The partners

Chinese workers—with shaven heads or broad, cone-shaped hats—appear among the laborers who are making wine in a California vineyard.

shared responsibility for the lease and the operation of a farm. In 1869, an observer described these enterprises: "We found the broad fields apportioned off and rented to separate companies of Chinamen who were working them upon shares—each little company having its own cabin. Teams [of draft animals] being furnished them, they do all the working, preparing the ground, seeding, tending the crop, and gathering the fruit, leaving nothing for the proprietor to do but to attend to the marketing, and to put into his own pocket half of the proceeds."

Despite the success of some tenant farmers, most of the Chinese who worked in agriculture were wage-earning laborers. One white farmer explained that he had used white laborers first, but he found that they worked for only a few days before they quit. "I then went to a Chinaman," he said, "and told him I wanted to contract for binding and stacking wheat. . . . Several hundred of them came. We had one or two hundred acres that had been reaped, and needed putting up very badly; and the next morning it was all stacked. The Chinamen did the work that night. They did the work well and faithfully, and of course we abandoned white labor."

The Chinese also worked in the vineyards and wineries of the Sonoma Valley. There Hungarian immigrant Colonel Agoston Harszthy, who came to be regarded as the father of the California wine industry, had hired Chinese laborers to clear land and plant grapevines on his Buena Vista Ranch. A visitor to Harszthy's winery in 1863 found Chinese working in the vineyards and also filling bottles with champagne, corking them, and wiring them shut. In addition, he saw Chinese workers blasting and excavating wine cellars.

By 1870, nearly one-fifth of all farm laborers in California were Chinese. The Chinese were especially numerous in Sacramento, Alameda, San Mateo, Yuba, Solano, Santa Clara, Yolo, and Tehema counties. Polish journalist Henryk Sienkiewicz reported that the work in the hop fields and fruit orchards of northern California was done "almost exclusively by hired Chinese." In 1893, a newspaper called the *Pacific Rural Press* acknowledged the contribution of the Chinese laborers: "The Chinese are the mainstay of the orchardist and thus far it must be said, form the only supply of labor which he can depend on. They are expert pickers and packers of fruit. It is difficult to see how our annual fruit crop could be harvested and prepared for market without the Chinaman."

Like the Chinese workers in industry, Chinese farm laborers were paid lower wages than whites. Chinese laborers received $30 a month; this was $10 to $20 less than white workers received. The Chinese were trapped in a system in which wages were based on race, with higher wages for whites. They could make ends meet on their lower wages only because

A Chinese worker at the Pacific American Fisheries Cannery in Bellingham, Washington. Such jobs were eventually closed to Chinese immigrants because of the hostility of white laborers.

45

A mob attacks Chinese workers in Rock Springs, Wyoming, in 1885.
Racial antagonism erupted into anti-Chinese riots throughout the West,
where Chinese immigrants were killed or driven away from their jobs.

they had left their families in China, where the cost of living was much lower than in the United States. Most workers were forced to keep their families in China because they could not support their wives and children in America. In addition to the pains of hard work and low pay, they suffered the loneliness of separation.

Chinese farm laborers did not always quietly accept what their employers offered them. In 1880, Chinese fruit pickers in Santa Clara County went out on strike, seeking higher pay. A few years later, new immigration laws cut the flow of Chinese newcomers. This reduced the supply of farm labor. Seeing that their labor had become more valuable, Chinese farm workers demanded higher wages. They even began to form unions, labor organizations that would represent their interests.

Chinese and white workers could have united to form stronger, more effective labor unions, but racial antagonism kept them apart. The Chinese had become targets of white resentment, especially during hard times. "White men and women who desire to earn a living," the *Los Angeles Times* reported in 1893, "have for some time been entering quiet protests against vineyardists and packers employing Chinese in preference to whites."

These protests were not always quiet. When economic times grew tough, the frustration of unemployed white workers erupted into violent anti-Chinese riots throughout California. From Ukiah to the Napa Valley, from Fresno to Redlands, the Chinese were beaten and shot. They were herded to railroad stations and loaded onto trains. The Chinese bitterly remember this expulsion as the "driving out."

Although Chinese laundry workers became a common sight in American cities, few people were aware that laundry work was not a traditional Chinese occupation. Chinese men in the United States turned to laundry work because it was one of the few opportunities open to them.

FACED WITH HOSTILITY FROM WHITE WORKERS IN THE mines, factories, and fields, many Chinese decided to become self-employed. They opened stores, restaurants, and especially laundries. Chinese laundries were a common sight as early as the 1850s. A journalist who visited California in 1853 commented on the hardworking Chinese laundrymen: "What a truly industrious people they are! At work, cheerfully and briskly, at ten o'clock at night."

In 1870, there were 2,900 Chinese laundry workers in California, and one out of every 17 Chinese was a laundry worker. Twenty years later, California had 6,400 Chinese laundry workers; one in every 12 Chinese worked in a laundry. Nearly half of the establishments listed in Sacramento's *Directory of Chinese Business Houses* for 1878 were laundries. Chinese laundries sprang up all over the United States, not just in California. By 1900, one of every four employed Chinese men in the country was a laundryman.

The "Chinese laundryman" was an American phenomenon, not a transplant from China. "The Chinese laundryman does not learn his trade in China; there are no laundries in China," said Lee Chew, a laundry worker who came to America in the early 1860s. "The women there do the washing in tubs and have no washboards or flat irons. All the Chinese laundrymen here were taught in the first place by American women just as I was taught." In China, explained another migrant, laundry work was a "woman's occupation," and men did not "step into it for fear of losing their social standing."

Why did Chinese men in America enter this line of work? Unlike a store or a restaurant, a laundry could be opened with a small amount of money, perhaps $75 to $200. The requirements were simple: a stove, trough, dry-room, sleeping apartment, and a sign. Also, a Chinese laundryman did not need to speak much English to operate his business. "In this sort of menial labor," said one, "I can get along speaking only 'yes' and 'no.'" He could also manage without knowing numbers. "Being illiterate, he could not write the numbers," another laundryman said of a fellow operator. "He had a way and what a way! See, he would draw a circle as big as a half dollar coin to represent a half dollar, and a circle as big as a dime for a dime, and so on. When the customers came in to call for their laundry, they would catch on to the meaning of the circles and pay accordingly."

But Chinese laundrymen were also pushed into laundry work because it was one of the few opportunities open to them. Explained Lee Chew, "Men of other nationalities who are jealous of the Chinese have raised such a great outcry about Chinese cheap labor that they have shut him out of working on farms or in factories or building railroads or making streets or digging sewers. So he opens a laundry."

The "Chinese laundry" was a retreat from the mainstream economy, with its limited opportunities for Chinese workers. Chinese men opened laundries not because they wanted to wash and iron clothes, but because laundries gave them a chance to work. "You couldn't work in the cigar factories or the jute or woolen mills any more—all the Chinese had been driven out," old Chinese men later remembered sadly. "About all they could be was laundrymen or vegetable peddlers then."

In a laundry there were usually two workers, one doing the washing and a second the ironing. Work began about seven o'clock in the morning on Monday. "The man who irons does not start in till Tuesday," Lee Chew said, "as the clothes are not ready for him to begin until that time. So he has Sundays and Mondays as holidays. The man who does the washing finishes up on Friday night, and so he has Saturday and Sunday off. Each works only five days a week, but those are long days—from seven o'clock in the morning till midnight."

"Ah, those days were hard ones," a retired laundryman sighed. "It is very hard to work at the laundry." Recalling the weight of the heavy iron, filled with red-hot charcoal, he added, "They don't call it the 'Eight-Pound Livelihood' for nothing." Another laundryman said, "I don't like this kind of life; it is not human life. To be a laundryman is to be just a slave. I work because I have to. I feel backaches all the time and headaches. I am not an old man yet, but I feel old." Their lives seemed to be measured by the pieces of clothing they

A Chinese store in Arizona. To avoid the hostility of white industrial workers, many Chinese opened their own shops, restaurants, and laundries.

51

washed and ironed. A Chinese song described the boredom and weariness of their workdays:

A lumber camp kitchen in the 1880s. Chinese immigrants often found work as cooks in labor camps or on ranches.

> One piece, two pieces, three pieces,
> The clothes must be washed cleanly,
> Four pieces, five pieces, six pieces,

The clothes must be ironed smoothly. . . .
You say laundry is really cheap work;
And only the Chinamen are willing to be so low. . . .
Really, I, too don't believe there is a future
in it,
Washing people's sweat with your own blood
and sweat.
Would you do that? Wouldn't you do that?
Year after year, with a nostalgic drop of tear;
Deep at night, by the flickering laundry light.

Working and living in their small shops, the laundrymen felt caged. "Nobody can imagine such a life as ours in the 'Golden Mountain,'" said one of them. "I have been confined in this room for more than two years. Sometimes I feel so lonesome in this small jail, I just want to go back to China."

The laundrymen washed and ironed clothes for white miners and workers who frequently mistreated and harassed them. "We had to put up with many insults and some frauds," complained Lee Chew, "as men would come in and claim parcels that did not belong to them, saying they had lost their tickets, and would fight if they did not get what they asked for." In the mining country, Lee Chew said, "we made plenty of money in gold dust, but had a hard time, for many of the miners were wild men who carried revolvers and after drinking would come into our place to shoot and steal shirts." Running a laundry was not an easy life, but it gave many Chinese immigrants a livelihood.

A Louisiana plantation in 1871. After slavery was abolished, southern planters hoped that Chinese laborers would take the place of black field-workers.

Chapter Five

Mississippi Fields and Massachusetts Factories

MOST OF THE CHINESE IN 19TH-CENTURY AMERICA lived in the West. But there were Chinese elsewhere in the United States, including the South and the East. In the South, the Chinese found themselves in a society that had traditionally been made up of two races, whites and blacks. Southerners were used to thinking of people in terms of their race. Many whites in the South had long regarded black people as their inferiors, and they viewed the Chinese in the same way.

The era of Reconstruction, in the years following the Civil War and the end of slavery, was a troublesome time for southern planters. When slavery was abolished, they lost control of the black laborers who had once been forced to work in their cotton fields. Now many of them hoped that the Chinese would fill the role that had once been occupied by the slaves. "Emancipation has spoiled the negro and carried him away from the fields of agriculture," the editor of a Mississippi newspaper said in 1869. "Our prosperity depends entirely upon the recovery of lost ground, and we therefore say let the Coolies come."

That same year, a southern planters' convention in Memphis, Tennessee, urged southerners "to look to the teeming population of Asia for assistance in the cultivation of our soil and the development of our industrial interests." A labor contractor who had imported 30,000 Chinese laborers into California offered to bring Chinese workers to the South.

Planters quickly saw that the hardworking Chinese could be used as models for black workers. Planters in

Louisiana and Mississippi imported Chinese laborers and pitted them against black workers. They praised the Asian workers for outproducing the black workers, and they used the threat of hiring more Chinese laborers to keep the black workers from demanding higher pay or better working conditions. A southern governor frankly explained, "Undoubtedly the underlying motive for this effort to bring in Chinese laborers was to punish the Negro for having abandoned the control of his old master, and to regulate the conditions of his employment and the scale of wages to be paid him."

In 1870, a Mississippi newspaper reported the successful introduction of Chinese laborers: "Messrs. Ferris and Estell, who are cultivating on the Hughs place, near Prentiss, recently imported direct from Hong Kong, a lot of Chinese, sixteen in number, with whom as laborers, they are well pleased." A traveling reporter vividly described the 140 Chinese workers on a plantation near New Orleans:

> Mounting horses and spreading our umbrellas, we rode out a mile or more through the fields, past countless negroes and mule-teams ploughing, to the spot off by themselves where the picturesque heathens were hoeing cane. . . . The Chinamen went on with their work, hoeing the young cane, and doing it very carefully and precisely. Occasionally they would look up at us, but in a very stolid, careless way. Ah Sing approached and greeted us with a polite, "Hallo, how do?" On learning that we were well, he observed . . ., "Belly hot to-day."

The wife of a Louisiana planter wrote to her daughter that the Chinese were very good workers, who only took half a day off for holidays: "Yesterday was their Christmas day and they asked for half the day and had prepared themselves a good dinner." One day, she continued, one of the "China-men" had come into the yard and asked for her. "I went to the porch to see what he wanted. He took off his hat, got down on his knees, and bowed himself his head touching the ground four times very stately then got up. I thought he was drunk but it was a mark of respect he was showing."

But the Chinese did not stay on the plantations. As early as 1871, the *New Orleans Times* noted that the Chinese preferred working in urban businesses and factories to the "plodding work of the plantations." By 1880, there were 50 Chinese in Mississippi, 133 in Arkansas, and 489 in Louisiana. Ninety-five of them lived in New Orleans, working as laundrymen, cigarmakers, shoemakers, cooks, and wood-carvers. By then, however, the southern planters had over-thrown the federal policies of Reconstruction. They had regained much of their political power over the black workers, and they quickly lost interest in Chinese labor.

In 1870, while southern planters were experiment-ing with Chinese labor, New England businessmen were attentively watching the small town of North Adams, Massa-chusetts. After a long ride on the recently completed trans-continental railroad, 75 Chinese workers had arrived in North Adams to work in one of its shoe factories. They had been brought there to help break a strike by Irish laborers.

Since 1840, North Adams had grown from an iso-lated rural village into an industrialized town. A magazine article called it "one of the busiest little towns, humming and smoking with various industries, and nestled in the most picturesque and mountainous part of the valley of the Housa-

*This shoe factory in
North Adams, Massachusetts,
was the scene of an industrial
experiment when the first
Chinese factory workers were
introduced to the East Coast
in 1870. Factory owners
pitted Chinese workers
against white workers,
fueling racial resentment.*

tonic." Almost a third of its residents were European immigrants, mostly Irish. North Adams had 38 factories—cotton mills, woolen mills, carriage manufactories, paper mills, and shoe factories.

The owner of one of these busy factories, Calvin T. Sampson, had established "A Model Shoe Factory." His factory made more than 300,000 pairs of shoes each year. The local press praised it as a successful business "built up from small beginnings, by persistent energy, industry, economy, and judgment." In reality, Sampson's success was based on machinery and the strict control of his workers. Three years after founding his factory in 1858, Sampson adopted a new type of machine to stitch leather. The new technology increased efficiency and profits. A single machine did the work of six men and saved Sampson two cents on every pair of shoes made. But this mechanical marvel also reduced workers from skilled craftsmen to low-paid, unskilled machine operators.

Sampson's increasing use of machinery instead of craftsmen reflected what was happening throughout New England. Many factory owners were replacing workers with equipment. The workers, hoping to protect themselves from labor-eliminating machines and low wages, founded a labor union called the Secret Order of the Knights of St. Crispin. This union was founded in 1867, and within three years it was the largest organization of its kind in the United States. It had 50,000 members, including many workers in the shoe factories of Massachusetts.

In 1870, the Crispins at Sampson's shoe factory went on strike, demanding higher wages and an eight-hour work-day. Sampson fired the striking workers and tried to hire replacements from a nearby town. But the local workers refused to take the jobs of the men who had been fired, so Sampson decided to declare war on the Crispins and drive a "wedge" into the conflict.

The "wedge" was a group of Chinese workers from San Francisco. Sampson had already been thinking about hiring Chinese labor. A year before the strike, a shoe manu-facturers' magazine had condemned the Crispins and urged employers to import Chinese workers to break strikes. Shortly after the strike began at his own factory, Sampson sent his superintendent to San Francisco to bring back some Chinese workers. He agreed to pay a labor supplier a commission for the Chinese workers and also to pay their fare to Massachusetts. Each worker would earn $23 a month for the first year and $26 a month for the next two years, plus lodging and fuel. In turn, the laborers agreed to work for three years. They would buy their own clothing and food.

The 75 Chinese workers reached North Adams in June of 1870. Their arrival was an occasion of great interest in the East. "A large and hostile crowd met them at the depot, hooted them, hustled them somewhat, and threw stones at them," one newspaper reported. Policemen marched the new-comers to dormitories at Sampson's factory, where they were placed behind locked and guarded gates—partly to protect them and partly to keep them under tight control. A few days later, a Boston paper announced, "They are with us! the 'Celestials'—with almond eyes, pigtails, rare industry, quick adaptation, high morality, and all—seventy-five of them— hard at work in the town of North Adams."

Another newspaper predicted that "the invading army of Celestials" would free Sampson from "the cramping tyr-anny of that worst of American trades-unions, the 'Knights of St. Crispin.'" White workers as well as white employers watched with interest as Sampson reopened his factory.

They did not have to wait long for results. Within three months, the Chinese workers were producing more shoes than an equal number of white workers had made. The success of Sampson's experiment was widely reported in the press. One editor wrote, "The Chinese, and this especially annoys the Crispins, show the usual quickness of their race in learning the process of their new business, and already do creditable hand and machine work." Another editor visited Sampson's factory and said he had never seen "a busier, more orderly group of workmen."

Scribner's Monthly magazine praised the Chinese workers for always coming to work on Monday because, unlike white workers, they did not get drunk on Sunday. Furthermore, they did not waste time on "idle holidays." The *Scribner's* writer added that the quality of their work was "fully equal to that of the Crispins." Chinese labor had increased Sampson's profits. A week's production cost $840 less with Chinese than with white workers. This added up to a savings of $40,000 a year. These figures inspired the *Scribner's* writer to calculate, "There are 115 establishments in the State, employing 5,415 men . . . capable of producing 7,942 cases of shoes per week. Under the Chinese system of Mr. Sampson, a saving of

Chinese laborers were barred from entering the United States by the Chinese Exclusion Act, which was passed in 1882 and renewed in 1892. The Chinese who were already living in the country had to obtain certificates of residence like this one, which belonged to Ah Chung, a laborer in Tucson, Arizona.

The entry into industry of Chinese laborers, such as this ironworker at a smelting plant, raised questions for 19th-century America. Could the Chinese blend in with American society? What should their role be?

$69,594 per week, or say $3,500,000 a year, would be effected, thus revolutionizing the trade."

Sampson's daring action discouraged white workers in other North Adams shoe factories from going on strike. Ten days after the Chinese workers arrived, four other companies forced striking laborers to return to work with 10% wage cuts by threatening to replace them with Chinese. One reporter said that "Chinese labor should be hailed with warm welcome" because it would help break white unions. The Chinese, he concluded, could be the "final solution" to the labor problem in America.

Other factory owners were impressed by Sampson's experiment. Three months after the arrival of the Chinese in North Adams, a New Jersey businessman brought 68 Chinese laborers to Belleville, New Jersey, to work in his steam laundry. Like Sampson, he had secured the workers through a labor supplier in San Francisco. Eventually he employed 300 Chinese workers—not just for their labor but also to end strikes by his Irish workers. And a knife factory in Beaver Falls, Pennsylvania, hired 70 Chinese laborers to bring striking white workers under control. Within a year, the company employed 190 Chinese workers.

The promise of Chinese labor had been proven in the mines, railroads, farms, and factories of the West. Its potential had been tested in the South and the East. But from the very beginning, the Chinese represented a dilemma. No one knew how they would fit into American society. "What we shall do with them is not quite clear yet," one journalist wrote of the Chinese in 1869. "How they are to rank, socially, civilly, and politically, among us is one of the nuts for our social science students to crack,—if they can." What role would the Chinese come to play in America? And what would be the future of white workers if industrial development depended more and more on Chinese labor? These questions became urgent as the 19th century drew to a close.

The character Ah Sin from Bret Harte's poem "The Heathen Chinee." Harte claimed to respect the Chinese, yet his poem and several stories promoted an image of Chinese people as deceptive, sly, and outlandish—an image that encouraged discrimination against Asian immigrants.

AH SIN WAS HIS NAME.

Chapter Six

"The Heathen Chinee"

WHAT WAS TO BECOME OF THE CHINESE IN AMERICA? One possible answer was to turn them into a caste, a group socially separated from other Americans. The Chinese would be an army of migrant laborers, forced to be foreigners forever. They would form a distinct group within American society, kept apart by race and regarded as inferior. Unlike white immigrants such as the Irish, Italians, and Poles, the Chinese would never be allowed to melt into the American mainstream.

One person who supported this idea was Charles Crocker, the superintendent of the Central Pacific Railroad, who had employed thousands of Chinese workers on the transcontinental railway. "I do not believe they are going to remain here long enough to become good citizens," Crocker told a legislative committee, "and I would not admit them to citizenship." Crocker and others like him thought that Chinese people should be allowed to enter the United States to work temporarily, but they would have to go back to China before they could become settled in American communities. They would be replaced by other workers fresh from China, who would be sent home in their turn. The Chinese would not have a future as citizens in the United States. They would fill the need for workers in American factories without making the country less white. Anti-Chinese laws, economic exploitation, and racial antagonism would make the Chinese eager to leave America after a short time. Under this system, the Chinese would remain forever foreign, always "strangers" in America.

Today most people would denounce such a plan as intolerably racist. In the 19th century, however, it was widely discussed. White Americans generally believed that the United States should be made up of people who shared the same racial and cultural background. To them, "American" meant "white."

The idea that America should be a white country was in the air long before the Chinese arrived. It shaped the fate of the blacks and the American Indians. Blacks had been imported as slave labor and freed only after a long, costly battle. Indians had been systematically driven off their land; many of them were killed. Their histories showed that the majority of whites in 19th-century America did not regard other races as their equals.

When the Chinese came to California, the question of race and national identity was again raised. Many whites associated the Chinese with blacks. Shortly after the Civil War, the *New York Times* warned that both the newly freed blacks and the newly arrived Chinese were threats to the American political system: "We have four millions of degraded negroes in the South . . . and if there were to be a flood-tide of Chinese population—a population befouled with all the social vices, with no knowledge or appreciation of free institutions or constitutional liberty, with heathenish souls and heathenish propensities . . . we should be prepared to bid farewell to republicanism." The *San Francisco Chronicle* also compared the Chinese "coolie" to the black slave, claiming that both were dangerous to free labor.

As the Chinese migrants discovered, white people quickly turned their stereotypes of black racial qualities into stereotypes of "Chinese" characteristics. Calling for a ban on

Chinese immigration, a San Francisco newspaper warned, "Every reason that exists against the toleration of free blacks in Illinois may be argued against that of the Chinese here." White workers called the Chinese "nagurs," and a magazine cartoon depicted a Chinese man as a bloodsucking vampire with slanted eyes, a pigtail, dark skin, and thick lips. Like blacks, the Chinese were described as heathen, morally inferior, savage, childlike, and lustful. Chinese women were condemned as a "depraved class" and said to resemble Africans.

Like blacks, the Chinese were viewed as threats to white racial purity. As early as 1661, Maryland had passed the first law prohibiting marriage between whites and blacks. By the 19th century, most states had laws against racial intermarriage. But California's law was especially designed to include the Chinese. A California legislator warned that only "the lowest" whites would intermarry with Chinese. In 1880, state lawmakers made it illegal for a white person and a "negro, mulatto, or Mongolian [Chinese]" to obtain a marriage license.

Whites also compared the Chinese with the American Indians. A California newspaper editor declared that the winning of the West from the "red man" would be in vain, if whites were now to turn the conquered land over to a "horde of Chinese."

The association between Indians and Chinese suggested one way to solve the "Chinese Problem." A former governor of New York asked, "We do not let the Indian stand in the way of civilization, so why let the Chinese barbarian?" In a letter published in the *New York Times,* he proudly declared: "Today we are dividing the lands of the native Indians into

67

states, counties, and townships. We are driving off from their property the game upon which they live, by railroads. We tell them plainly, they must give up their homes and property, and live upon corners of their own territories, because they are in the way of our civilization. If we can do this, then we can keep away another form of barbarism which has no right to be here."

A senator from Alabama also compared the Chinese with American Indians. Both were "inferior" and subject to federal government control. The government, he argued, should do to the Chinese what it had already done to the Indians: put them on reservations.

All three groups—blacks, Indians, and Chinese—were nonwhite. Racism was behind much of the hostility

Chinese girls at a church school in California in the early 1880s. As Chinese immigrants began to raise families in the United States, the nation debated the future of the Chinese in America.

toward them. In 1854, the California Supreme Court turned racial prejudice into law in the case of *People v. Hall.* A year before, a white man named George W. Hall and two others were tried for murdering a Chinese man, Ling Sing. During the trial, one Caucasian and three Chinese witnesses testified against the white men. The jury found Hall guilty, and the judge sentenced him to be hanged. But Hall's lawyer appealed the verdict, arguing that the Chinese witnesses should not have been allowed to testify against Hall. A California law said that "no black or mulatto person, or Indian, shall be permitted to give evidence in favor of, or against, any white person." The question now was whether Chinese were also barred from giving evidence against whites. The California Supreme Court decided that they were. It freed Hall, declaring that "Chinese and other people not white" could not testify against whites.

In 1859, the California superintendent of education applied the color line to the public schools. He warned that the integration of blacks, Indians, and Chinese would ruin the schools, saying, "The great mass of our citizens will not associate on terms of equality with these inferior races; nor will they consent that their children should do so." A year later, the California legislature segregated the schools. Public money could be kept from any school that admitted non-whites.

President Rutherford Hayes talked about the "Chinese Problem" in 1879. The "present Chinese invasion," he argued, "should be discouraged. Our experience in dealing with the weaker races—the Negroes and Indians . . . —is not encouraging. . . . I would consider with favor any suitable measures to discourage the Chinese from coming to our shores."

Bret Harte, author of
"The Heathen Chinee."
Despite the poem's
immense popularity,
he disparagingly
called it trash.

The movement to exclude the Chinese was growing stronger. The exclusionists thought that the "strangers" from Asia posed a greater threat than blacks and Indians. The Chinese were believed to be more intelligent and competitive than blacks; and they were increasing in number, rather than decreasing as the Native Americans were.

Those who wanted to keep the Chinese out of America feared that Chinese laborers would take white workers' jobs and force whites into poverty. During the 1870s, white workers expressed this anxiety in a popular song:

O workingmen dear, and did you hear
The news that's goin' around?
Another China steamer
Has been landed here in town.
Today I read the papers,
And it grieved my heart full sore
To see upon the title page,
"O, just 'Twelve Hundred More!'"
O, California's coming down,
As you can plainly see.
They are hiring all the Chinamen
and discharging you and me;
But strife will be in every town
Throughout the Pacific shore,
And the cry of old and young shall be,
"O, damn, 'Twelve Hundred More.'"

A play called *The Chinese Must Go*, by Henry Grimm of San Francisco, put the racial fears of white workers on the stage. Two Chinese characters, Ah Coy and Sam Gin, conspire to destroy white labor. Ah Coy says, "By and by white man catchee no money; Chinaman catchee heap money; Chinaman workee cheap, plenty work; white man workee dear, no work—sabee?" According to Grimm, white workers had reason to be alarmed, for the sinister Chinese were planning to take away their jobs and even their country. One of the white characters in the play describes the Chinese workers as vampires, sucking the life out of Uncle Sam.

The most powerful expression of anti-Chinese fears and anxieties was a poem called "The Heathen Chinee," by Bret Harte, a well-known author. The poem was published in 1870, and it instantly became immensely popular. Newspapers across the country reprinted it, and the phrase "heathen Chinee" passed into common usage in white America.

Harte's poem was timely. The transcontinental railroad had been completed in 1869, and thousands of Chinese, released from railroad jobs, were moving into the cities. At the same time, the railroad was bringing thousands of white workers from the East to California in search of jobs. More and more, whites in California saw the Chinese as competitors in the crowded job market. By the end of 1870, there were three workers—two white and one Chinese—for every job in San Francisco. But fear of Chinese labor competition was not confined to the West. Chinese workers had been hired in the Massachusetts shoe factory just three months before Harte's poem appeared. The poem was a focus for nationwide anti-Chinese fears. White Americans laughed at it, but nervously.

"The Heathen Chinee" describes a card game between a Chinese man named Ah Sin and an Irish man named William Nye. Determined to beat his opponent, Nye has cards stuffed up his sleeves—yet, even with his extra cards, the white man

As anti-Chinese feeling rose, some businessmen catered to their customers' racial prejudices. These Seattle restaurants assured patrons that they did not employ Chinese cooks or waiters.

loses time and again. Ah Sin has a "childlike" smile, but the reader learns

> That for ways that are dark
> And for tricks that are vain
> The heathen Chinee is peculiar.

Suddenly, Nye catches Ah Sin cheating. Ah Sin, too has cards hidden in his sleeves. Upon discovering this, Nye punches his opponent and shouts, "We are ruined by Chinese cheap labour."

The message of the poem is not clear. While it stereotypes the Chinese as cunning tricksters, it portrays Nye as a cheater too. Yet Harte's readers carried away a lasting image of the "peculiar" ways of the "heathen Chinee." They remembered Ah Sin's deceptiveness and slyness, and his ability to "ruin" white labor in America. Ironically, Harte regarded himself as a friend of the Chinese. He regretted the racist effect of his poem, telling a friend, "Perhaps you can have little respect for a poet who wrote such trash as the *Heathen Chinee.*"

After the poem was published, Bret Harte continued to write about the Chinese in America, but again his message was mixed. He objected to the mistreatment of the Chinese by whites. But he also contributed to anti-Chinese racism by portraying the Chinese as "heathens" and threats to white America. This contradiction appears in two of Harte's short stories, "Wan Lee, the Pagan" and "See Yup."

"Wan Lee, the Pagan" begins with a visit to the Chinese merchant Hop Sing, a "grave, decorous, handsome gentleman" with a pigtail. Harte reports that Hop Sing's warehouse has a "mysterious foreign odor." Hop Sing offers tea and a snack of sweetmeats from a "mysterious jar" that looks as if it might contain "a preserved mouse."

The principal character in the story is Wan Lee, a 12-year-old San Francisco boy. Wan Lee is impish and good at "imitation." He is also "superstitious" and wears around his neck "a hideous little porcelain god." Hop Sing explains that the boy has spent "perhaps too much" time around American children. Wan Lee falls in love with a white girl. Their relationship is a touching one. "Bright," "cheery," and "innocent," the girl awakens "a depth in the boy's nature that hitherto had been unsuspected." When she goes to school, Wan Lee walks behind her, carrying her books and defending himself against the racist attacks of "Caucasian Christian" boys. He also makes beautiful presents for her, and she returns his kindness. She reads and sings to him; she gives him a "yellow" ribbon for his pigtail to match his "complexion"; and she takes him to Sunday school.

They get along very well—"this little Christian girl, with her shining cross hanging around her plump, white, little neck, and this dark little Pagan, with his hideous porcelain god hidden away in his blouse." But tragedy awaits them. At the end of the story, Wan Lee is killed during two days of anti-Chinese mob violence in San Francisco—"two days when a mob of her citizens set upon and killed unarmed, defenseless foreigners, because they were foreigners and of another race, religion, and color, and worked for what wages they could get."

The story condemns the "Christian" murderers of Wan Lee, but again Harte was sending a double message to white America. The Chinese were described as unfortunate victims of white hatred and cruel racism. Yet they were also depicted as mice-eaters, "mysterious," "pagan," "dark," "impish," "superstitious," "yellow," and dangerous to white labor and white racial purity. Although Harte said that he disapproved of injustices against the Chinese, he created images that made Chinese people seem alien and inferior to whites.

The story "See Yup" contains the same contradictory meanings. In this story, See Yup is a laundryman in a small mining town. He is a "heathen" who exudes a "peculiar odor"—half ginger, half opium—called the "Chinese smell." See Yup is victimized by whites, whom Harte describes as "ignorant and brutal." White boys tie See Yup's pigtails to a window, and white miners take their dirty clothes to his laundry and pick up their clean clothes without paying for them. The unhappy target of racial abuse, See Yup knows he can find no justice in the courts.

One Saturday, See Yup enters the Wells Fargo office and asks the clerk to send a bag of gold dust valued at $500 to San Francisco. He had gathered the gold, it seemed, in an abandoned mine. He sends gold to San Francisco three Saturdays in a row, and the clerk at the Wells Fargo office spreads the news that See Yup has made a strike. The white miners then organize themselves into a committee and visit See Yup's mine. In two hours, they watch See Yup and his fellow Chinese miners take $20 worth of gold dust from the sand and gravel. The work is being performed in the "stupidest, clumsiest, yet *patient* Chinese way." And the white miners exclaim, "What might not white men do with better appointed machinery!"

The white miners force See Yup to sell his mine for a meager $20,000. After he sells, See Yup leaves town. The

PACIFIC CHIVALRY.
Encouragement to Chinese Immigration.

Thomas Nast, one of the nation's best-known political cartoonists during the 19th century, savagely satirized California's anti-Chinese spirit in an 1869 cartoon.

white miners take over the mine and bring in new machinery. Some gold is found in the first week, but nothing is found the next week. Then the miners learn what has happened. See Yup had borrowed $500 in gold dust from a friend, sent the gold to San Francisco, and had Chinese runners secretly return it to him so that he could send it out twice more. After he was forced into selling his mine, he sprinkled a little gold dust at the mine, and then he disappeared with his $20,000.

Once again, Harte's point was not entirely clear. The white miners certainly got what they deserved. But See Yup was a trickster. The character created by Harte reflected a widespread belief that the Chinese were clever, tricky, and clannish, ready to conspire against white Americans. "We knew," Harte's narrator remarks in the story, "that the Chinese themselves possessed some means of secretly and quickly communicating with one another." See Yup was a threat to the white men because of his so-called "typical" Chinese characteristics. It was this image of the Chinese—outwardly humble but secretly sly and resourceful—that alarmed many white Americans.

Bret Harte's poems and stories were intended to entertain and amuse readers. But "the Chinese question" was also the subject of serious writings. A social critic and writer named Henry George examined the issue during the 1860s and 1870s.

George published his analysis of the "Chinese Problem" in the *New York Tribune.* He pointed out that the steamship had made it possible for large numbers of Chinese to migrate to the United States. These Chinese were crowding into the labor market of California and becoming the new "peons" of industry. "The superintendents of the cotton and woolen mills on the Pacific prefer the Chinese to the other operatives," George noted, "and in the same terms the railroad people speak of their Chinese graders, saying they are steadier, work longer, require less watching, and do not get up strikes or go on drunks."

Comparing the Chinese workers of modern industry with the black slaves of earlier years, George warned that the Chinese were more dangerous. Blacks brought to America were "simple barbarians with nothing to unlearn." They were "docile" and capable of accepting white ways. But the Chinese migrants could not blend into white society. Their ancient civilization had given them "habits of thought" quite unlike those of the European whites. These yellow workers were a "population born in China, reared in China, expecting to return to China, living while here in a little China of its own, and without the slightest attachment to the country—utter heathens, treacherous, sensual, cowardly and cruel." To George, the Chinese immigrants would always be aliens in America. Unlike European peasants, the Chinese immigrants could not be made into Americans. Immigrants from China would remain Chinese.

These views were shared by many white Americans, who called for laws to ban or at least limit the immigration of Chinese. In 1882, the U.S. Congress passed the Chinese Exclusion Act, which prohibited the entry of Chinese laborers. During the public discussion of the law, one newspaper editor noted that the law would appeal to white workers, especially the "hard-working Bill Nyes" of the Pacific Coast—a reference to the character created by Bret Harte in "The Heathen Chinee."

Congress had little real reason to worry about Chinese immigrants threatening white labor. When the Exclusion Act was passed, the Chinese made up a mere 2,000th of 1% of the U.S. population. The act really reflected fears that had little to do with the Chinese. It was Congress's answer to the growing conflict between white workers and employers. By banning the Chinese, Congress hoped to satisfy the working class, which was growing increasingly angry.

Something seemed to have gone wrong with the American economy. Since the beginning of English settlement, there had always been plenty of land and jobs in America. The biggest problem for employers had always been the need for more workers. But suddenly, in the late 19th century, society experienced a bitter new reality: unemployment. Joblessness became a national crisis. Times of prosperity were followed by intense and painful recessions, when wages dropped and workers lost their jobs. These recessions produced workers' strikes and riots.

Against this background of economic and social strife, Congress made it unlawful for Chinese laborers to enter the United States. In addition, the Chinese who were already in the country were barred from becoming citizens. Support for the law was overwhelming. Even in states where there were few or no Chinese, people supported the anti-Chinese legislation. Lawmakers believed that banning the Chinese would calm the dissatisfied white workers and heal the rifts within white society.

The Exclusion Act brought about a sharp decline in the Chinese population in America, from more than 100,000 in 1880 to about 60,000 in 1920. Congress had tried to answer the "Chinese question" by making laws to keep the Chinese out. The Chinese, however, did not let the exclusion laws pass without a fight. They protested against discrimination and struggled to win civil rights.

*Politicians beat a Chinese immigrant in a cartoon from 1882—the year
in which anti-Chinese feeling culminated in the Chinese Exclusion Act,
a restrictive new immigration law.*

THEY ARE PRETTY SAFE THERE.

When Politicians do Agree, their Unanimity is Wonderful

"GIVE IT TO HIM, HE'S GOT NO VOTE NOR NO FRIENDS!"

Chapter Seven

The Chinese Struggle for Civil Rights

AS EARLY AS THE 1850s, A CHINESE MIGRANT HAD WRITten to a friend: Why did whites treat the Chinese with "contempt"? Many Chinese had been killed by "lawless wretches," and Chinese witnesses of the crimes had not been allowed to testify in courts. The root of this problem was racism. "Now, what injury have we Chinese done to your honorable people," the writer angrily questioned, "that they should thus turn upon us and make us drink the cup of wrong even to its last poisonous dregs?"

To the Chinese, white prejudice was both uninformed and insulting. In an open letter to California governor John Bigler, published in a newspaper in 1852, Norman Asing criticized the governor for an anti-Chinese message to the state legislature. He described the Chinese cultural heritage:

> The effect of your late message has been thus far to prejudice the public mind against my people, to enable those who wait the opportunity to hunt them down, and rob them of the rewards of their toil. . . . We would beg to remind you that when your nation was a wilderness, and the nation from which you sprung *barbarous,* we exercised most of the arts and virtues of civilized life; that we are possessed of a language and a literature, and that men skilled in science and the arts are numerous among us; that the productions of our manufactories, our sail, and workshops, form no small commerce of the world. . . . We are not the degraded race you would make us.

To protect themselves from prejudice, the Chinese turned to their organizations. The most important of these, the Chinese Six Companies, challenged the discriminatory laws and protested against anti-Chinese harassment and violence. In an 1876 letter to President Ulysses Grant, the Chinese Six Companies declared that the United States had always welcomed immigrants from all countries to its shores. The Chinese had responded by crossing the ocean to America. Noting the contributions of the Chinese, the Chinese Six Companies asked: "Are the railroads built by Chinese labor no benefit to the country? Are the manufacturing establishments, largely worked by Chinese, no benefit to this country? Do not the results of the daily toil of a hundred thousand men increase the riches of this country?"

A year later, the Chinese Six Companies denounced the mob violence committed against the Chinese in "this *Christian civilization.*" The organization warned the mayor of San Francisco that self-defense was the right of all people, adding that if the city's Chinese quarter were attacked, its inhabitants would defend themselves "to the last extremity."

Time and again, the Chinese went to the courts in their struggle for civil rights. Insisting on the right of Chinese immigrants to become citizens, Chan Yong applied for citizenship in San Francisco's federal district court in 1855. Chan Yong, the local newspapers noted, was more "white" in appearance than most Chinese, but the court denied him citizenship, ruling that the 1790 Naturalization Law restricted citizenship to "whites" only and that the Chinese were not "white."

Seven years later, the Chinese won a victory in the courts. Ling Sing sued the San Francisco tax collector, chal-

lenging the $2.50 tax that each Chinese had to pay in California. In *Ling Sing v. Washburn*, the California Supreme Court ruled that while the Chinese could be taxed like residents, they could not be set apart for special taxes. This ruling was significant. Ling Sing had overturned a state law on the grounds that it violated the U.S. Constitution.

The *Ling Sing* decision showed that federal protection was needed to ensure civil rights for the Chinese. International politics offered the Chinese community a chance to be heard.

The directors of the Chinese Six Companies, the largest and most active of many associations formed by Chinese settlers in America. These organizations took a leading role in the Chinese fight for civil rights.

The United States and China were negotiating a treaty in 1868, and the Chinese Six Companies urged that the treaty contain provisions to protect the Chinese in the United States. They contacted a San Francisco lawyer who was involved in the treaty negotiations and explained to him that federal laws were necessary to "free" the Chinese in the United States from "wrongs" and to protect Chinese lives and property. They pointed out that federal protection of Chinese property would also encourage Chinese investments in the United States and promote American trade with China.

The outcome of the treaty negotiations was a major victory for the Chinese Six Companies. The 1868 Burlingame Treaty recognized the "free migration and emigration" of the Chinese to the United States as visitors, traders, or "permanent residents." It also gave Chinese people in the United States the right to "enjoy the same privileges, immunities, and exemptions in respect to travel or residence, as may there be enjoyed by the citizens or subjects of the most favored nation."

Buoyed by their success with the Burlingame Treaty, Chinese merchants sought federal action to abolish discriminatory state laws. In 1869, representatives of the Chinese community met with a congressional committee in San Francisco. Merchant Fung Tang asked the congressmen to give the Chinese the civil rights that had been guaranteed to them by the Burlingame Treaty. He also asked for federal protection from state injustices, especially the foreign miners' tax and the fact that Chinese witnesses could not testify in the courts. Tang argued, "We think your special tax, collected *only* from Chinese miners, is not according to our treaty with your government. We are willing to pay taxes cheerfully, when

The
Chinese
Struggle
for
Civil
Rights

taxed equally with others. . . . Most of all—we feel the want of protection to life and property when Courts of Justice refuse our testimony, and thus leave us defenseless, and unable to obtain justice for ourselves."

Again the Chinese struggle for civil rights was effective. The 1870 Civil Rights Act, well known for its protection of blacks, also contained provisions for the civil rights of the Chinese. It gave all persons in the United States the right to make and enforce contracts, to sue, to give evidence, and to enjoy the same rights under law that "white citizens" enjoyed, even if other laws and statues said otherwise. Furthermore, immigrants from one country could not be made to pay taxes that were not imposed equally on all other immigrants.

But guarantees of protection by treaty and by federal law had little or no effect on what actually happened in society. The Chinese remained vulnerable, victims of discrimination and violence. Blamed for all the troubles of the American working class, the Chinese suffered from racial attacks. They had to flee from American boys who screamed "God Damn Chinamen" and threw rocks at them.

"When I first came," Andrew Kan told an interviewer in 1924, 44 years after his arrival, "Chinese treated worse than dog. Oh, it was terrible, terrible. At that time all Chinese have queue and dress same as in China. The hoodlums, roughnecks and young boys pull your queue, slap your face, throw all kind of old vegetables and rotten eggs at you."

"The Chinese were in a pitiable condition in those days," recalled one immigrant in his account of San Francisco Chinatown during the 1870s. "We were simply terrified; we kept indoors after dark for fear of being shot in the back. Children spit upon us as we passed by and called us rats."

Merchants in San Francisco's Chinatown lived in fear of persecution from whites. "We were simply terrified," one said, "We kept indoors after dark."

The Chinese saw that the source of their oppression was racism, for they were treated very differently from the European immigrants. "Up to 800,000 Europeans enter the United States per year, yet the labor unions hardly cared," the Chinese Six Companies noted. "A few thousands of the Chinese arrivals would irritate American workers . . . and European immigrants get citizenships and voting rights often immediately after their arrival in the United States."

*The
Chinese
Struggle
for
Civil
Rights*

After the Chinese Exclusion Act was passed in 1882, laundryman Lee Chew claimed that "it was the jealousy of laboring men of other nationalities—especially the Irish—that raised all the outcry against the Chinese. No one would hire an Irishman, German, Englishman or Italian when he could get a Chinese, because our countrymen [were] so much more honest, industrious, steady, sober, and painstaking. Chinese were persecuted, not for their vices, but for their virtues."

Although they suffered from racial and ethnic persecution, some Chinese viewed other groups in terms of stereotypes. Lee Chew, for example, had absorbed some typical American ethnic prejudices. He maintained that the Irish were criminals, the Italians were dangerous, and the Jews were unclean and ignorant. He complained, "Yet they are all let in, while Chinese, who are sober, or duly law abiding, clean, educated and industrious, are shut out. . . . More than half the Chinese in this country would become citizens if allowed to do so, and would be patriotic Americans."

Immigrants with white skins did not remain "strangers" in America the way Asians did. A Chinese immigrant named Ginn Wall painfully understood this reality. He had come to the United States in the 1870s to work on the railroad. He brought his wife, hoping they would be able to make a home for themselves in California. Many years later he cursed America for denying him the fulfillment of his dream. "Let's just fold up here," he told his son. "You come with me and we'll go back home. This is a white man's country. You go back to China when you make your money, that is where you belong. If you stay here, the white man will kill you."

By the late 1870s, there were enough Chinese-owned businesses in the western states for Wells Fargo & Company to publish a separate directory listing them.

Other Chinese laborers shared Wall's apprehension and fear. Few Chinese men had brought their wives with them. Chinese people in the United States were generally afraid to raise families and make their homes in America. In 1855, a Chinese merchant in San Francisco explained that the Chinese had been "warned" not to come to America. As a result, they did not find "peace in their hearts in regard to bringing families." Noting how the Chinese were victims of racial violence and robbery, he sadly concluded, "If the rabble are to harass us, we wish to return to our former homes."

A depiction of a crowd of angry whites pelting Chinese immigrants upon their arrival in San Francisco.

Many did return. Between 1850 and 1882, 330,000 Chinese migrants entered the United States. Of these, nearly half went back to China. But thousands of Chinese sojourners decided to stay—or found they could not return to their homeland.

For many Chinese migrants, America turned out to be not Gold Mountain but a mountain of debt. "From the proceeds of a hard day's toil, after the pay for food and clothes, very little remains," explained the Chinese Six Companies in a protest against the foreign miners' tax in the late 1850s. Chinese migrants had borrowed money for their passage, or perhaps had sold all of their property to come to America. Now they felt bitter because they could not earn enough to go back to China.

In 1876, the Chinese Six Companies again complained in a message to Congress:

> Many Chinamen have come; few have returned. Why is this? Because among our Chinese people a few in California have acquired a fortune and returned home with joy. . . . They have expected to come here for one or two years and make a little fortune and return. Who among them ever thought of all these difficulties? Expensive rents, expensive living. A day without work means a day without food. For this reason, though wages are low, yet they are compelled to labor and live in poverty, quite unable to return to their native land.

Two young girls in San Francisco's Chinatown. Chinatowns grew rapidly in San Francisco and other cities during the late 19th century; they were not simply ethnic communities but symbols of the Chinese future in America.

Chapter Eight

Putting Down Roots

NOT ALL OF THE CHINESE MIGRANTS DREAMED OF RE-
turning to their homeland. Although they considered themselves sojourners, not permanent settlers, Chinese migrants
showed signs of settlement from the very beginning. They
created Chinatowns in Sacramento, Marysville, Stockton,
Fresno, Los Angeles, and especially San Francisco. During the
1850s, the Chinese community in San Francisco had 33
general merchandise stores, 15 medicine shops, 5 restaurants,
5 herb shops, 5 butcher stores, 3 boarding houses, and 3 tailor
shops. This was the start of a distinctive, bustling community
that continued to grow.

White Americans were fascinated by the Chinese
quarter. They thought it was exotic and colorful. "The majority of the houses were of Chinese importation," observed
a traveler, "and were stores, stocked with hams, tea, dried fish,
dried ducks, and other Chinese eatables, besides copper pots
and kettles, fans, shawls, chessmen, and all sorts of curiosities.
Suspended over the doors were brilliantly-colored boards
covered with Chinese characters, and with several yards of red
ribbon streaming from them; while the streets thronged with
Celestials, chattering vociferously as they rushed about from
store to store."

A Chinese immigrant who arrived in San Francisco in
1868 found a thriving Chinatown "made up of stores catering
to the Chinese only." The Chinese were "all in their native
costume, with queues down their backs." The street fronts of
stores were open, letting groceries and vegetables overflow
onto the sidewalks. Chinese vegetable peddlers filled the
morning streets "in loose pajamalike pants and coats carrying

two deep baskets of greens, fruits, and melons, balanced on their shoulders with the help of a pole."

Nine years later, the Chinese quarter of San Francisco was six blocks long, running from California Street to Broadway. All day and into the night, the streets were crowded with Chinese. According to one visitor, the Chinese had shaven heads and neatly braided queues. They sauntered "lazily along, talking, visiting, trading, laughing, and scolding in the strangest, and, to an American, the most discordant jargon." Here and there they gathered in groups on street corners. They sometimes amused themselves at "the expense of some party of 'white people,' who, passing through 'Chinatown' to see the sights," provided a source of entertainment to the Chinese.

Everywhere in Chinatown, signboards in Chinese characters gave the stores and shops poetic names. Adorning the entrances of wholesale houses were signs for Wung Wo Shang ("everlasting harmony, producing wealth"), Tung Cheung ("unitedly prospering"), Wa Yung ("the flowery fountain"), and Man Li ("ten thousand profits"). Apothecary shops had signboards that read, "The hall of the approved medicines of every province and of every land." Restaurants had signboards describing the culinary delights they offered: "Fragrant almond chamber," "Chamber of the odors of distant lands," or "Fragrant tea chamber." A store that sold imported goods carried the signboard Chai Lung Shing ("abundant relief").

Gambling saloons bore signboards full of promise: "Get rich, please come in," "Straight enter the winning doors," or "Riches ever flowing." On the glass windows and doors of their stalls, opium dealers pasted red cards announcing "Opium dipped up in fractional quantities, Foreign smoke in broken parcels, No. 2 Opium to be sold at all times." The walls of stores bore scrolls that stated, "Profit coming in like rushing waters, Customers coming like clouds," or "Ten thousand customers constantly arriving, Let rich customers continually come."

Organizations abounded in the Chinatowns. Tongs, or secret societies, were part of urban life in China, and they were present almost from the beginning of Chinese settlement in America. In Guangdong, the tongs were underground anti-government movements; in Chinese America, they gave

A Chinese theater in San Francisco in the 1880s. Women sat apart from the men in the curtained boxes to the right of the stage.

support and security to people who felt themselves to be outsiders.

"We are strangers in a strange country," said a tong member. "We must have an organization (tong) to control our country fellows and develop our friendship." For example, a laundry worker said he decided to join a tong because he believed tongs encouraged the Chinese to help each other while they were in "a strange land."

Tongs offered their members protection. "Occasionally members of the tongs use their organization to take advantage of non-members of tongs," said a Chinese. "For example, a Chinese leased a building and found it necessary to raise his rent to pay for the advanced rent on his new lease; the renters threatened to bring trouble to the non-tong member who held the lease, unless he let them have the old rate of rent." Meeting the needs of immigrants, tongs multiplied in the United States and took over the vice industry. They came to control the opium trade as well as gambling and prostitution in the Chinese communities.

Despite the unsavory nature of some of their activities, the tongs had high-sounding names. The On Leong Society ("Chamber of Tranquil Conscientiousness") and the Kwang-tek-Tong ("Chamber of Far-Reaching Virtue") were prostitution organizations. Tongs were colorful and visible in Chinatown. After the death of a tong leader, the tong would hire bands for the funeral, "both American and Chinese, and have a long parade—not just for mourning, but to show its glory."

Chinese immigrants also formed *fongs*, composed of close family and village members, and clans, larger groupings of village associations. The fongs maintained clubhouses that

To whites, Chinatown was exotic and colorful, a bit of foreign culture in the middle of an American city. Sidewalk stalls and shops open to the streets gave passersby a view of the varied goods—here, toys, dried fruits, and peanuts.

served as residences and social centers. The clans established temples, sent letters to the villages in China, and shipped home the bodies or bones of the deceased. In San Francisco Chinatown, they also provided a police and garbage service.

Larger than the fongs and clans were the district associations, based on the regions from which the migrants had originated. These associations were responsible for receiving the migrants. They provided the newcomers with housing and helped them find jobs. The district associations also administered the "credit-ticket" system, checking the migrants who returned to China to make certain all their debts had been paid.

In San Francisco during the 1850s, the district associations were the Sze Yup, Ning Yeung, Sam Yup, Yeong Wo, Hop Wo, and Yan Wo; they later organized themselves into the Chung Wai Wui Koon, or Chinese Six Companies. This

*Paul Grenbeaux's moody photograph of a San Francisco Chinatown
alley at night captures the feeling of mystery with which white
tourists viewed the first Chinese communities.*

organization helped settle conflicts among Chinese people from different districts, and it provided educational and health services to the community. The leaders of the Chinese Six Companies were merchants who dealt with the city's white business community. They could express the Chinese point of view to public officials, and they also found influential Americans to advise and speak for the Chinese population.

Gradually, the Chinese were creating their own communities in America. They built altars to honor their gods: Kwan Kung, god of literature and war; Bak Ti, god of the north; Hou Wang, the monkey god; and Kwan Yin, goddess of mercy. They celebrated traditional holidays. During Chinese New Year in January or February, they first did their *Dah Faw Hom Muy,* or housecleaning. "Everything is cleansed to prepare for welcoming the coming year," journalist A. W. Loomis reported in 1869. "The house is almost turned inside out; ceiling, floors and furniture are scrubbed."

The house could not be cleaned again until after the celebration, or else the good fortune arriving with the new year would be swept away. "Oh yes—we cleaned the house upside down," a Chinese immigrant remembered. "You know it was good luck to have plenty at the start of the New Year. We couldn't buy too much, but a bit of everything. And then there would be oranges and lishee [gifts of money wrapped in red paper for good luck]. We didn't have money for the lishee—we used dried nuts for money."

Then the Chinese ushered in the New Year with traditional dances, parades, and firecrackers. During the celebration, whites joined the festive throngs in Chinatown. "The merchants," said a San Francisco resident, "appear highly delighted to see and to welcome all of our citizens whom they

97

A father and two sons in San Francisco's Chinatown, dressed in the traditional formal garb of a prosperous Chinese family. The designs on the boys' tunics represent the scepter of the Buddha; they are symbols of long life.

can recognize as friends, and all with whom they have had any kind of business connections." The Chinese offered liquor and cigars to the whites. As soon as the clock tolled off the last minute of the departing year, firecrackers exploded in a roaring, crackling din, filling entire streets with columns of smoke and sheets of flame, turning the ground red with shreds of exploded paper, and frightening away the evil spirits for the coming year. A Cantonese poem described this time of celebration:

New Year's Day starts a new calendar year.
The scent of spice fills the air beyond the front
   door.
Everywhere, we Chinese sojourners greet each other
   with auspicious sayings.
In joyous laughter,
We wish good luck to others, and to ourselves.
May this year be prosperous for all walks of life;
So that, clothed in silk, we can together bid the
Flowery Flag [America] farewell.

In the spring, the Chinese held their Pure Brightness Festival, or *Qing Ming.* This was a memorial day for the Chinese in America. Unable to visit the family graves in China, they went to local Chinese cemeteries, where they prayed before spirit shrines. In the fall, the Chinese celebrated the Moon Festival to thank the gods for good harvests. During this celebration, they enjoyed moon cakes, moon-shaped pastries filled with delicacies such as salted duck egg yolks and sweetened soybean paste.

For recreation, the Chinese attended the Chinese theater. The first Chinese play in America was presented in 1852 at the American Theatre in San Francisco by 123 actors of the Hong Fook Tong. In 1879, a Chinese theater was built in the city. It held audiences of up to 2,500 people; admission tickets cost 35 cents. During performances, the Chinese men sat on benches in the gallery. Smoking cigars and cigarettes, eating mandarin oranges and Chinese melon seeds, they escaped for a few hours into a world of Chinese music and drama.

A prostitute in San Francisco. Many of the Chinese women who came to America in the early years of immigration were forced into prostitution.

Chapter Nine

Chinese Women in America

AMONG THE CHINESE IMMIGRANTS, MEN GREATLY OUT-numbered women. The Chinese women who came to America found themselves in a world of men. In 1852, there were 1,700 Chinese men to each Chinese woman in California. Eighteen years later, there were still 14 men to each woman.

Chinese women worked in a variety of occupations. They were housekeepers, servants, laundresses, seamstresses, shoemakers, cooks, miners, and fisherwomen. But overwhelmingly, in the early years, Chinese women were prostitutes. In the 1870 census, 61% of the 3,536 Chinese women in California had their occupations listed as "prostitute." Most of the Chinese prostitutes were working for employers, under contracts like this one signed by Xin Jin:

> The contractee Xin Jin became indebted to her master/mistress for food and passage from China to San Francisco. Since she is without funds, she will voluntarily work as a prostitute at Tan Fu's place for four and one-half years . . . to pay this debt. There shall be no interest on the money and Xin Jin shall receive no wages. At the expiration of the contract, Xin Jin shall be free to do as she pleases. . . . If Xin Jin becomes sick at any time for more than 15 days, she shall work one month extra; if she becomes pregnant, she shall work one year extra. Should Xin Jin run away before her term is out, she shall pay whatever expense is incurred in finding and returning her to the brothel.

Chinese prostitutes worked in mining outposts, railroad camps, agricultural villages, and Chinatowns. Some of them, dressed in fancy clothes and wearing jewelry, worked in high-class brothels. "And every night, seven o'clock, all these girls were dressed in silk and satin, and sat in front of a big window," recalled Lilac Chen, who had been brought to America in 1893 by a brothel owner, "and the men would look in and choose their girls who they'd want for the night."

Most of the prostitutes, however, worked in lower-grade brothels or in "cribs"—small street-level compartments facing dim alleys, with bars or heavy screens over their windowed doors. Dressed in cotton tunics and trousers, women peered out from the windows, promising men pleasure for 25 or 50 cents. A common slogan was "Lookee two bits, feelee floor bits, doee six bits." Two bits is an old-fashioned term for a quarter. The slogan meant that a customer could look at a woman for 25 cents, touch her for 50 cents, or have sex with her for 75 cents. The prostitutes were fed two or three times a day. Their dinner usually consisted of rice and a stew of pork, eggs, liver, and kidneys.

Prostitutes made a lot of money for their owners. Little better than slaves, many of them became opium addicts. The drug gave them relief from the abuse and degradation they encountered every day. "My owners were never satisfied, no matter how much money I made," one prostitute complained. When they were angry, her owners would often beat her with wooden clubs; once they threatened her with a pistol. "My last mistress was very cruel to me," another prostitute said; "she used to whip me, pull my hair, and pinch the inside of my cheeks." A Chinese folk song urged prostitutes to seek husbands and a safer life:

Prostitution ruins the body most harmfully.
Come ashore, the sooner the better.
My advice is to get hitched to a man, and don't
    ever forget, dear young lass:
It's no shame to have a decent meal with plain tea.
All in all—
You'd also gain a husband.
We've all witnessed the frequent raids of brothels
    in the Golden Gate;
You need not to worry about these roughnecks once
    you live with a man.

A prostitute's life was dangerous, and sometimes short. Disease was a constant threat. Syphilis and gonorrhea were widespread. Some prostitutes were beaten to death by their customers or owners. Others committed suicide by taking an overdose of drugs or by drowning themselves in the San Francisco Bay.

A woman named Wong Ah So was luckier. She was at a "party given by the Tong men" where "slave girls" sat and drank with the men. "Suddenly I saw a friend of my father's come in, a man who had seen me less than a year ago," she recalled. "Although I was all dressed up so grand he recognized me, and the first chance he had, he came and asked me, 'Are you not so and so's daughter?'" Ten days later, thanks to his efforts, Wong Ah So was rescued and taken to a Christian mission.

The number of Chinese prostitutes in California dropped after 1870. Only 24% of the 3,171 Chinese women in the state were listed as prostitutes in the 1880 census. But the number of Chinese women described in the census as

Born in China in 1853, Polly Bemis survived a harsh life to become a western heroine. Her family sold her to bandits, who sent her to America as a slave. She was auctioned off to a saloon keeper in Idaho, where a man named Charlie Bemis won her in a card game and then married her. Polly and Charlie Bemis homesteaded along the Salmon River, and by the time of her death in 1933, Polly was a beloved member of the community.

"housekeepers" had increased. Chinese men had begun bringing their wives with them to America, or arranging to have women sent from China to become their wives. For example, a Chinese man who came to California when he was about 15 years old found work in the Sacramento River delta in levee construction. "Levee building was very hard work, but at least it was steady," his grandson later explained. "After my grandfather had decided to settle down in the Sacramento Delta, he went back to China on a sailboat to marry, and then brought his wife over here."

In 1862, at the age of 18, Gee-Hee Chin came to America. He worked in a lumber mill in Washington and saved his earnings. Within a few years, he sent for a wife and got her a job as a cook at the mill. In 1875, she gave birth to their son, Lem, believed to be the first Chinese baby born in the Washington Territory.

In 1869, journalist A. W. Loomis reported the case of "a wife coming all the way alone across the stormy sea" to be with her husband: "Friends at home besought her not to do a thing so in conflict with Chinese custom; the husband and his relatives in this country, when they heard of her purpose, wrote entreating her not to expose herself to the hardships and perils on the sea, and to the trials which would be liable to befall her here; but she answered that where the husband was there she had a right to be." She came to California, where she supported herself and her child by sewing garments and making cigarettes while her husband worked for a mining company.

In Washington, California, and elsewhere, Chinese families gradually formed as the men left mining and railroad construction for more stable pursuits such as farming and shopkeeping. The fishing industry in Monterey, California, encouraged the formation of Chinese families. Nearly half of the Chinese inhabitants in the fishing village of Point Alones, for example, were women. The village was organized into companies, but most of these companies were actually families: "Man Lee Company, three men and three women; Sun Sing Lee Company, three men, two women and three children."

As early as 1876, in a letter to President Ulysses Grant, the Chinese Six Companies noted the presence of "a few hundred Chinese families" in the country, and added, "There are also among us a few hundred, perhaps a thousand, Chinese children born in America."

Increasingly, Chinese men wanted to find wives and settle down. But they discovered that sometimes getting a wife could be vexatious and expensive. Fook Sing of Downieville,

California, went through a trying ordeal. He had heard about a Chinese woman named Min Que who was in Wadsworth, Nevada. On July 25, 1874, he sent a telegraph to Kaw Chung in Wadsworth: "Don't you let her go. I will come tomorrow and see her. I want to bring her to Downieville to live with me. What time does the train start? Answer quick."

The next day Fook Sing sent another message to Chung: "I will start for Wadsworth today and meet her. . . . Tell her to wait for me to come and if she wants to go I will let her. Don't care. Answer." But the woman went off with or was taken by another man. On August 12, Ah Tom sent a telegram to Ting Yeu of Downieville: "Fook Sing's woman has gone to Marysville." The next day the disappointed and anxious Fook Sing sent two telegrams to Sing Lung in Marysville. The first one read: "Bring woman up right away will pay three hundred dollars. Answer." The second read: "Is man who took woman there? Answer."

At 11 in the morning on that same day, Sing Lung wired Tie Yuen in Downieville: "Tell Fook Sing Min Que is here. What you going to do? Answer quick." Fook Sing had found the woman, but would Min Que agree to marry him? At 4 in the afternoon, Sing Lung telegraphed Fook Sing: "She wants you to come right away and get warrant with officer, friends will help. You don't be afraid. We will get her sure." Fook Sing rushed to Marysville, and on August 15, he wired Tie Yuen: "I saw the woman but have not arrested her. Send marriage certificate." Immediately Tie Yuen responded: "Will send the certificate next stage."

Fook Sing, it seems, was able to get himself a wife, but he was one of the lucky few. "In all New York there are less than forty Chinese women," laundryman Lee Chew com-

mented bitterly, "and it is impossible to get a Chinese woman out here [to the United States] unless one goes to China and marries her there, and then he must collect affidavits to prove that she is really his wife. That is in the case of a merchant. A laundryman can't bring his wife here under any circumstances."

A Chinese wedding party in Idaho City, Idaho, poses for the camera.

Most Chinese men were trapped in a womanless world. "You know Chinese no allowed to marry white girl in California and Oregon. Only in Washington and up here make lots of trouble," Gen Woo of Seattle told an interviewer. Protesting the laws against the entry of Chinese women, Woo asked, "What Chinese going do for wife?"

Cut off from the women of their homeland, a few Chinese men developed relationships with white women. In 1886, the San Francisco Board of Supervisors reported several white-Chinese couples living in Chinatown. Among "the white women of Chinatown," Lee Chew reported, were "many

Social workers, as well as the Chinese Six Companies and other civic groups, strove to aid Chinese prostitutes, who were generally treated as slaves by the employers who held their contracts. These girls were rescued by missionaries.

excellent and faithful wives and mothers." Chinese men in New York, wrote a Chinese journalist, were married to "Irish, German, or Italian wives," most of them "poor working girls." He added, "The Chinamen often make them better husbands then men of their own nation, as quite a number of them who ran away from their former husbands to marry Chinamen have openly declared. The Chinaman never beats his wife, gives her plenty to eat and wear, and generally adopts her mode of life. Their children speak the English language, and adopt the American ways and dress."

On Sundays and holidays, the streets of Chinatown filled with men
seeking amusement and companionship. Many Chinese men in
America knew loneliness because they did not have families.

Chapter Ten

A World of Bachelors

FOR THE OVERWHELMING MAJORITY OF CHINESE MEN in America, the future would not include the possibility of a family. "Pathetic the lonely bachelors stranded in a foreign land," reflected a Chinese migrant in a poem. On Sundays, most Chinese men had no families to take on outings. They had "no *homes* in this country," said the Reverend Otis Gibson of San Francisco, and nearly all the common laborers lived on the streets on Sundays simply because they had "nothing to do, and nowhere else to go."

Sitting at tables or lying on beds, they read novels. "Yes, go to theater," a waiter at a Chinese restaurant replied when asked about his free time. "When I no work? I sleep. Sometimes gamble a little." At night and during the weekends, men played mah-jongg, fan tan, and other games. "Gambling is mostly fan tan," reported Lee Chew, the laundryman, "but there is a good deal of poker, which the Chinese have learned from Americans and can play very well. They also gamble with dominoes and dice."

One migrant, a cook and houseboy, said, "No get lonely for home China, many China boys all same one family. Sometime have holiday. Put on Merican hat, shoe, tie, all same White man, walk to Stockton have good time." Men also sought escape in the brothels or the opium parlors. Inhaling deeply from ivory opium pipes, they "mounted the dragon" and rode into fantastic worlds far away from their dull, lonely reality.

Mostly, however, the men spent their leisure hours in the back rooms of Chinese stores. There "all Chinese came," a migrant recalled. "Not just relatives. They all just like to get

together. They talk together. . . . Sometimes they even get
some idea from China. Our village had something to do—they
send a letter over here, we get together and talk it over—and
send it back. We communicate, see, otherwise you're alone.
You know nothing."

A uniquely Chinese-American social institution, the
store was a center of life in the Chinese community. There
the men could buy Chinese foods, books in Chinese, firecrackers, incense, ceremonial paper, Chinese herbs, and other fa-
miliar goods. There they escaped from the "strangeness and
fierceness of their everyday world," and recalled "happier days
at home when they crowded the village inns . . . to drink tea
and exchange gossip, or to listen to vagrant minstrels chant
ballads." In the back rooms of the stores, men spent many
pleasant hours telling Chinese folktales. Many were ghost
stories, like the one about "The Sound of the Slippers":

> In China many years ago the father of a certain woman
> died. . . . The daughter had cared a great deal for him
> and when he died she grieved deeply. Not long after
> his death she was awakened one night by a familiar
> sound, the sound of her father's slippers walking
> across the floor. She was not afraid of ghosts or of
> darkness, so she got up to look, but she could not
> discover anything unusual. Many nights after that she
> heard the sound, always at the same time, and always
> she would wake up and investigate, but never did she
> discover what it meant.
>
> Shortly afterwards the daughter was married and her
> husband took her over here, to America. She arrived
> in America and had forgotten all about the sound of

the slippers. But one day she heard it again, here in her new home in America. She was very much surprised at this. She did not think it strange when she heard it in China. But here in America! The sound was exactly the same as that she had heard when she lived in her little house in the village. And, even today, ever so often always at the same hour, she hears it and she knows, that it is the sound of her dead father's slippers scratching across the floor.

A San Francisco opium den around 1900. "Mounting the dragon," as they said, men inhaled the narcotic smoke and escaped their dreary surroundings for a time.

Gathered around a stove in the back room of a store, Chinese men challenged each other at chess and checkers, played musical instruments, listened to records, and read newspapers. Some of them also taught each other English, struggling through an English-Chinese phrase book compiled in San Francisco in 1875. The phrases in this book show the experiences, anxieties, and hopes that made up the everyday lives of the Chinese in 19th-century America:

He took it from me by violence.

The men are striking for wages.

He claimed my mine.

When will the lease expire?

He cheated me out of my wages.

He was choked to death with a lasso, by a robber.

Can I sleep here tonight?

Have you any food for me?

She is a good-for nothing huzzy.

The passage money is $50 from Hong Kong to California.

The steamer will leave to-morrow.

How long have you been in California?

She is my wife.

An unmarried man is called a bachelor.

I received a letter from China.

The United States have many immigrants.

The immigration will soon be stopped.

The back rooms were also information centers where the men found out what was happening around town and also in China. Public notices were written on "tablets of red paper and posted beside the door." Chinese newspapers were available, and interpreters were on hand to conduct negotiations and adjust differences with "the outside world." The store served as a community post office. Store owners used their writing skills to write letters for illiterate Chinese workers, and mail from China was sent to migrants in care of the stores. One sojourner received a letter from his mother. It was a wailing reminder to fulfill his obligations:

> I hear that you, ———, my son, are acting the prodigal. . . . For many months there has arrived no letter, nor money. My supplies are exhausted. I am old; too infirm to work; too lame to beg. Your father in the mines of the mountains suffers from a crushed foot. He is weak, and unable to accumulate money. Hereafter, my son, change your course; be industrious and frugal, and remit to me your earnings; and within the year let me welcome home both your father and yourself.

She had also written to an older relative, whom she had appointed to act as the young man's guardian:

> I hear that my son is playing the prodigal, being idle, or spending his earnings for unnecessary articles of clothing and in other forms of self-indulgence. I authorize you, his near relative and senior in years, to strenuously admonish him. If moderate chastisement fails, then call to your aid one or more of your brothers (relatives) and sorely beat him, not pitying his body.

Many of the sojourners dreamed of going home but were unable to do so. One migrant worked hard and saved his money, but he lost the money when a friend in Oregon

A brick wall in Chinatown served as a community bulletin board, with notices of jobs, announcements of important local events, and news from China.

invested it without his consent. "Because you took away that money," he wrote to his friend, "I could not return home. I came to America—to labor, to suffer, floating from one place to another, persecuted by the whites, for more than twenty years. . . . Do you know that both the old and the young at my home are awaiting me to deliver them out of starvation and cold?"

Another migrant, who had been in America for two decades, was scolded by his brother in a letter: "Because of our family's poverty, you went out of the country to make a living. You still haven't made any money during all of these twenty years? I am afraid that you are Americanized and totally forget about us."

Something had happened to these men and to thousands of other Chinese immigrants in the new land. They had come to America full of hope, searching for Gold Mountain, but in the end they found themselves "eating bitterness." For many of the Gold Mountain men, the venture was a sad failure.

My life's half gone, but I'm still unsettled;
I've erred, I'm an expert at whoring and
    gambling.
Syphilis almost ended my life.
I turned to friends for a loan, but no one took
    pity on me.
Ashamed, frightened—
Now, I must wake up after this long nightmare. . . .

In America, the Chinese were forced to become "strangers." They had left their homeland to escape its limitations, but they found new limitations in America. Economic pressures—the demands of white employers and ethnic antagonism from white workers—kept them from being treated as equals. So did the widely held view of America as a white society. The Chinese were denied equal opportunities and discriminated against by the law. "They call us 'Chink,'" complained a laundryman. "They think we no good! America cut us off. No more come now, too bad!"

Determined to find some kind of Gold Mountain in the new land, the immigrants had built one for themselves. They created their Chinatowns, and they fought for their civil rights in the larger society. They learned about law and democracy, and they became involved in politics. The law kept them from becoming United States citizens, but they knew they were worthy of citizenship. "Since I have lived and made money in this country," Andrew Kan argued in 1924, after 44 years of working in the United States, "I should be able to become an American citizen."

Before they came to America, the Chinese did not realize how they would affect the new land—or how it would affect them. Years after their arrival, they could marvel at what they had achieved and what they had become. Mostly peasants in the old country, they had become pioneering prospectors

A scribe writes letters for immigrants to their families in China. Such ties were precious, but as time went on many immigrants realized that they would not be returning to the land of their birth. They had become Chinese Americans.

in the foothills of the Sierra Nevada, railroad workers in the granite mountains of California and the salt deserts of Utah, agricultural laborers in the orchards of California and the cotton fields of Louisiana, enterprising farmers in the San Joaquin and Sacramento valleys, factory workers in San Francisco and Massachusetts, and laundrymen and shopkeepers from New York to Washington. "*Jo lui jai*," they said, "we worked like mules."

The Gold Mountain men and women created the world of Chinese America. They had brought greater racial and cultural diversity to American society. Although they had crossed a different ocean than the European immigrants, they knew they had earned their own claim to settlement—their claim to be Chinese Americans.

Chronology

1790	A federal law says that only "white" immigrants may become naturalized citizens of the United States.
1848	Gold is discovered in California.
1849	The California gold rush begins with the arrival of prospectors called "Forty-Niners," including 325 Chinese.
1850	California becomes a state.
1852	California enacts a foreign miner's license tax, which discriminates against Chinese miners.
1862	The California Supreme Court overturns a state law that had imposed a special tax on Chinese residents.
1865	The first Chinese workers are hired by the Central Pacific railway company.
1867	The Knights of St. Crispin, a white labor union, is formed in New England.
1868	The Burlingame Treaty between the United States and China guarantees protection for the civil rights of Chinese people in America.

1869   The transcontinental railway is completed at
        Promontory Point, Utah.
1870   The federal Civil Rights Act improves the
        legal status of the Chinese in America.
1882   The U.S. Congress passes the Chinese
        Exclusion Act, banning the immigration
        of Chinese.

Further Reading

Barth, Gunther. *Bitter Strength: A History of the Chinese in the United States, 1850–1870.* Cambridge: Harvard University Press, 1964.

Chan, Sucheng. *Asian Americans: An Interpretive History.* Boston: Twayne, 1991.

———. *This Bitter-Sweet Soil: The Chinese in American Agriculture, 1860–1910.* Berkeley: University of California Press, 1986.

Chen, Jack. *The Chinese of America: From the Beginnings to the Present.* New York: Harper & Row, 1981.

Chinn, Thomas, H. M. Lai, and Philip Choy. *A History of the Chinese in California.* New York: Chinese Historical Society, 1981.

Daley, William. *The Chinese-Americans.* New York: Chelsea House, 1987.

Gee, Emma, ed. *Asian Women.* Berkeley: Asian American Studies, University of California, 1971.

Hoexter, Corinne K. *From Canton to California: The Epic of Chinese Immigration.* Miami: Brown Book Company, 1976.

Hom, Marlon K., ed. and trans. *Songs of Gold Mountain: Cantonese Rhymes from San Francisco Chinatown.* Berkeley: University of California Press, 1987.

Jones, Claire. *The Chinese in America.* Minneapolis: Lerner Publications, 1972.

Knoll, Tricia. *Becoming Americans: Asian Sojourners, Immigrants, and Refugees in the Western United States.* Portland: Coast to Coast Books, 1982.

Lai, Him Mark, Genny Lim, and Judy Yung, eds. *Island: Poetry and History of Chinese Immigrants on Angel Island.* San Francisco: Chinese Culture Foundation, 1980.

Lee, Joann Faung Jean. *Asian American Experiences in the U.S.: Oral Histories of First to Fourth Generation Americans from China, the Philippines, Japan, India, the Pacific Islands, Vietnam, and Cambodia.* Jefferson, MO: McFarland Press, 1991.

Lyman, Stanford. *Chinatown and Little Tokyo.* New York: Assoc. Faculty Press, 1986.

McCunn, Ruthanne Lum. *Thousand Pieces of Gold.* San Francisco: Design Enterprises, 1981.

Mark, Diane, Mei Lin, and Ginger Chih. *A Place Called Chinese America.* Dubuque, IA: Kendall/Hunt, 1982.

Perrin, Linda. *Coming to America: Immigrants from the Far East.* New York: Delacorte, 1980.

Reimers, David M. *The Immigrant Experience.* New York: Chelsea House, 1989.

Takaki, Ronald. *From Different Shores: Perspectives on Race and Ethnicity in America.* New York: Oxford University Press, 1987.

———. *Iron Cages: Race and Culture in Nineteenth-Century America.* New York: Knopf, 1979.

Yung, Judy. *Chinese Women of America: A Pictorial History.* Seattle: University of Washington Press, 1986.

Index

African Americans, 55, 56, 66, 68, 70, 77, 85

Anti-Chinese laws, 47, 65, 66, 67, 78, 79, 84, 108

Belleville, New Jersey, 63

Bigler, John, 24, 81

Bing, Ah, 41

California, 17, 19, 21, 22, 23, 24, 25, 26, 29, 39, 41, 47, 49, 55, 66, 69, 70, 71, 77, 81, 83, 87, 89, 101, 103, 104, 105, 106, 107, 111, 112, 113, 114, 119

California gold rush, 17, 18, 19, 21

Cambodians, 18

"Celestials," 20, 22, 23, 32, 60, 91

Chew, Lee, 49, 50, 51, 53, 87, 108–9, 111

China, 17, 19, 20, 36, 47, 49, 65, 83, 87, 94, 99, 101, 104, 107, 111, 112, 113, 114, 115

Chinatowns, 20, 21, 85, 91–99, 102, 108, 117

Chinese agricultural laborers, 22, 41, 44, 45, 47, 49, 50, 63, 105, 119

  cigar makers, 37, 38, 50, 57

  farmers, 22, 41, 42, 43, 44, 49, 50, 63, 105, 119

  festivals, 97, 98, 99

  fishing industry, 105

  laundrymen, 49–53, 57, 63, 94, 101, 106, 107, 111, 117, 119

  laws against, 47, 65, 66, 67, 78, 79, 84, 108

  miners, 17, 18, 21, 22, 24, 25, 26, 27, 29, 37, 39, 41, 49, 63, 101, 105, 114, 118

  prostitution, 101–3, 111, 117

  railroad workers, 29–36, 41, 50, 63, 87, 105, 119

  religions, 97

role in labor disputes, 56,
   59–63
shoemakers, 36, 57,
   59–63
struggle for civil rights,
   79–89
theater, 99, 111
violence against, 47, 53, 60,
   74, 82, 85, 87
women, 49, 85, 101–9
Chinese Exclusion Act, 78, 79,
   87
Chinese Must Go, The (Grimm),
   70–71
"Chinese Problem," the, 67,
   69, 77, 78
Chinese Six Companies,
   82, 84, 86, 89, 95, 97,
   105
Chun-Chuen, Lai, 22
Civil Rights Act of 1870, 25,
   85
Civil War, 37, 55, 66
"Coolies," 20, 55, 66
Credit-ticket system, 20, 95

District associations, 95

East Indians, 18
1868 Burlingame Treaty, 84

Filipinos, 18
Fongs, 94, 95
Foreign miners' license tax, 24,
   25, 26, 84, 89

"Gold Mountain," 19, 20, 22,
   27, 53, 89, 117, 119
Grimm, Henry, 70

Guangdong, China, 18, 19,
   41, 93

Harte, Bret, 71, 72, 73, 74, 75,
   76, 77, 78
"Heathen Chinee, The"
   (Harte), 71, 72, 73, 78
Hmong refugees, 18
Hong Kong, China, 56,
   114

Idaho, 21

Japanese, 18

Koreans, 18

Ling Sing v. Washburn, 83
Loomis, A. W., 39

McDougal, John, 23
Marysville, California, 21, 26,
   29, 91, 106
Montana, 21

Native Americans, 67, 68, 69,
   70
North Adams, Massachusetts,
   57, 58, 60, 62, 63

Opium, 27, 74, 92, 93, 94,
   102, 111
Oregon, 41

People v. Hall, 69

Railroads, 29–36, 57, 65, 68,
   77, 82
Reconstruction, 55, 56, 57

Sacramento, California, 21,
    29, 45, 49, 91
Sampson, Calvin T., 58, 60,
    61, 63
San Francisco, California, 17,
    21, 22, 23, 27, 33, 36, 37,
    39, 59, 70, 71, 73, 75, 82,
    84, 88, 91, 95, 99, 101, 103,
    108, 111, 114
Secret Order of the Knights of
    St. Crispin, 59, 60, 61
Sing, Fong, 27
Slavery, 55, 66, 77

Stockton, California, 21, 91,
    111

Tenant farming, 42, 43, 44
Tongs, 93, 94
Transcontinental railroad line,
    29–36, 57, 65, 71

United States, 17, 23, 29, 35,
    47, 49, 55, 59, 65, 66, 82,
    84, 85, 86, 87, 88, 89, 94,
    107, 114, 117, 118

PICTURE CREDITS

RONALD TAKAKI, the son of immigrant plantation laborers from Japan, graduated from the College of Wooster, Ohio, and earned his Ph.D. in history from the University of California at Berkeley, where he has served both as the chairperson and the graduate advisor of the Ethnic Studies program. Professor Takaki has lectured widely on issues relating to ethnic studies and multiculturalism in the United States, Japan, and the former Soviet Union and has won several important awards for his teaching efforts. He is the author of six books, including the highly acclaimed *Strangers from a Different Shore: A History of Asian Americans,* and the recently published *A Different Mirror: A History of Multicultural America.*

REBECCA STEFOFF is a writer and editor who has published more than 50 nonfiction books for young adults. Many of her books deal with geography and exploration, including the three-volume set *Extraordinary Explorers,* recently published by Oxford University Press. Stefoff also takes an active interest in environmental issues. She served as editorial director for two Chelsea House series—*Peoples and Places of the World* and *Let's Discover Canada.* Stefoff studied English at the University of Pennsylvania, where she taught for three years. She lives in Portland, Oregon.